A Harsh Reality:
Iran Through the Eyes of a Teenager

Arya Nourizadeh

Preface
by
N. Nourizadeh

This book has been written by a young Iranian teenager living abroad. It shares his ideas and viewpoints on different subjects in Iranian politics such as human rights violations, women's rights abuse, inequality, child killing, the view of religions in Iran and other subjects that one might never link to politics, such as sports and more specifically, football. It also shares his viewpoints on many different past and present world conflicts such as the Russia-Ukraine conflict and the long feud between Israel and Palestine. Arya Nourizadeh tries to link many of these big-scaled issues and other small issues around the world with Iranian politics as he attempts to demonstrate his understanding of how to better a miserable Iranian society. He has written this book day by day, capturing his exact reactions and thoughts on that day to provide a unique perspective on how Iranian politics is and can be in the future. This is his first attempt at writing a literary piece.

To Nima, I love you. You kept on pushing me to write this.
Thank you.

I want to attempt to make Iran great again. I am not entirely sure how now, but one day, I will. The truth is, Iran deserves so much more, our country is slowly dying day by day and I cannot help but ask myself every single day; what have the people of Iran done to deserve such a fate?

First and foremost, a little bit about me. I am Arya Nourizadeh, and at the time that I am writing this, I am 19 years old. Young, right? I know. It doesn't take long in life to understand that your own country is run by a murderous government. I study Political Science because it interests me and can help me understand what is wrong with this cursed country and what is wrong with this forsaken world that we live in. I am writing this book for two reasons, the first is because I promised my father who also happens to be a writer and a translator, to write a book about Iran. The second reason is, I want to be one of the voices of the youth of Iran, who barely have any because of what the regime in Iran does to them. I live abroad, so it is a perfect opportunity to display what the Islamic Republic of Iran is like to non-Iranians. There may be little anecdotes here and there, where the focus will not necessarily lie on Iran, after all, the world is huge, and not everything should be revolved around Iran. I am learning day by day, something that will be said one day may not reflect my opinion in another.

It is almost time for the New Year, and this Iranian regime is still here. One of my best friends, Kayvan went to Iran and showed me plenty of pictures and videos of our beautiful country and it got me thinking that it is such a shame that Iran is constantly overlooked because of its politics. It is frustrating, especially when you live in a world where first impressions are key. Western media does a great job of depicting Iran as this terrible dangerous country when our people are just like any other people around the world where we want to live our lives in peace. Unfortunately, I have not been able to visit Iran since I was around twelve or thirteen years old. When anyone in Iran sends me pictures or videos, it is always refreshing to see them. My family has been insisting that I come there for years now, and although I would love to go there, life can be a little challenging at times. I do not wish to visit my country in the state that it is now. I want to see the land of Iran prosper. The people have endured this terrible regime for way too long. To understand the Iranian people's frustrations, you must understand the Islamic Republic as a whole. It came into power in 1979 after the overthrow of Iran's Shah, Mohammad Reza Pahlavi. Ayatollah Ruhollah Khomeini came into power. He was a religious leader who had an anti-Western ideology. For the next 42 years, the country of Iran would then transform, and everything even slightly Western would be forbidden. Furthermore, women in Iran are not treated well, they need to wear proper clothing.

In the eyes of the regime, women need to wear a long tunic over their clothes, and they are also required to cover their heads with a scarf. They cannot even enter stadiums to watch a game of football. How crazy is that? Do not worry, it gets even more ridiculous. Does this remind you of any past political regimes throughout history? I'll leave that up to you to find out.

It is the New Year today, and my resolution for 2022 is for the Iranian regime to go down. I am sure that I am not alone in adopting this resolution. With my father, I discussed Donald Trump and Iran's former military officer, Qasem Soleimani, who was killed in Iraq in 2020. We both agreed that America may not have needed to do that whatsoever. It was unlawful. The fact that the President of the United States had to go to such lengths to approach this situation is unacceptable. Something I have always wanted to do, weirdly enough, is to have a proper conversation with Donald Trump because he is a man that truly does intrigue me. He is a very questionable person, but my real opinion about him is that he is nothing more than an uneducated politician and a very annoying one. He does have a lot of supporters within America, and to my surprise, he does not have many abroad. Regarding Qasem Soleimani, a U.S. drone was targeting him and at that time, he was in Iraq awaiting to meet the country's Prime Minister when the drone hit him. It is an issue that was on the news for countless days. A huge shock for all of us, a lot of people were afraid that this would start a new war between both parties. Iran's murderous regime condemned the US government, vowing that there will be huge consequences for this assassination.[1] But here is something I want to teach you myself, everything that the Islamic Regime in Iran says should be taken with a grain of salt.

It is not worth entertaining the nonsense that comes out of their mouths. They are a bunch of thieves and liars who care only about themselves. IR is short for the Islamic Republic, and I will be using that throughout the book.

Today was the first day of classes at my university. My nerves were kicking in because I have never been to university. I had to buy this book by none other than Thucydides himself, titled "The History of the Peloponnesian War" and for homework, I had to read selections on justice, power, and human nature. I immediately picked up a phrase from the book that will stick with me for the rest of my life, for sure. Thucydides explained that politics is aimed at winning.[2] This sentence shows the harsh reality of politics.

It is a phrase that, although has been said thousands of years ago, is something that still applies in today's world. I can link this to the longtime feud between the United States of America and the Islamic Republic of Iran, where there is this battle of ideologies and egos that is ongoing, and it seems like it will just never stop. Both parties just want to win, both have done so much wrong over the years to get that win. Both have killed so many innocent people over the years and talking about it just makes me sick, very sick. I hate it. I hate it so much because ultimately at the end of the day, the ones that have suffered the most are innocent people that, as I mentioned before, just want to live their lives in peace. They got their lives stolen from them at the expense of their government. This is yet another reason I am writing this book. I want to shed light on some of the atrocities that exist in both Iran and the United States, I believe that people must know of Iran because generally, I believe that is a very misunderstood country that is completely ruined and outshined by its politics and its foreign policy.

Isn't it crazy that the people of Iran have not lived in peace since the revolution in 1979? Right after the revolution, there was the Iran-Iraq war that lasted eight years, and after that, the Western world was all on the IR's tail and since then the country has regressed every single day. Iran is now a country that has completely regressed, like I mentioned above, women are not even able to watch a game of football in the stadiums, and over the years, many women have attempted to do so, and some have even died from it, sadly. I am looking at you, Sahar Khodayari, whom I will never forget. She was a brave and intelligent girl who attempted to watch a football match disguised as a man when security officials took notice and arrested her. She ended her own life by burning herself to death, causing worldwide reactions.[3] Nevertheless, is this issue something that should occur in today's world? The IR has caused Iranians to live in a barbaric society and speaking against it can also get you killed. Throughout this book, I will also attempt to demonstrate other examples of just how our country has regressed throughout the reign of the Islamic Republic. You will probably notice that it will be a very reoccurring theme, because yes, that is how bad our country has become nowadays. Regarding Sahar Khodayari, it was a case that demonstrated the willingness of Iranian women concerning gender inequality and human rights. Her tragedy is something that would've been avoided in practically any other country.

It should be served as a reminder that women's rights are human rights, and everyone should be treated equally, regardless of their sexual orientation. Throughout this book, it will become clear that the Iranian government is not only misogynistic but also very barbaric.

I also have an International Relations class, which also contains some segments about the Islamic Republic of Iran. There are around a hundred people in the class, and I have never seen anything quite like this. But I finally had the courage the speak in front of the whole class. It took a lot of convincing and self-belief, but I finally did it. Speaking well is a crucial and fundamental part to become a politician. Usually, I am quite a shy person, but it was about Iran, and I will always raise my voice as loud as possible when it comes to my homeland, the professor was impressed, which made my day. I got to explain how misunderstood Iran was, and how unfortunate it is that I, a 19-year-old must stand up here just to talk about it. I am sure the professor knew about everything I said already, but what I hope most about is whether my classmates were listening to what I had to say. I am sure there are some Middle Easterners in the class who got to listen to what I said whether they agree with it or not. Iran, in the eyes of the Middle East, is a conflicted issue. Some believe the IR is doing the right thing. They believe that anti-West propaganda is a good thing, and it must keep going for as long as it can. There are others, who believe that the IR is a complete joke, and must be removed immediately. I heavily believe that the Islamic Republic is giving a bad image to Islam, although most Iranians are considered Shia Muslims and follow Islam a little bit differently from Sunni Muslims. Whatever it may be, the IR does a fantastic job at trying to convince people that whatever atrocities they are committing are part of the Islamic ideology, which of course, is false.

Last time I checked, Islam doesn't promote misogyny and other brutal ideologies that the IR believes in. They are simply using Islam as an excuse, and I find it disgusting.

Another interesting class I have is Canadian Politics, let's take a break from Iran for a second. I must admit I am quite intrigued at how multiple nations managed to make Canada what it is today. It gives Canada this sense of uniqueness, in my opinion.

I still firmly believe to this day that Canadian politics is badly run. The current Liberal government does not know what they are doing. I believe that they only care about money, just like almost all other governments around the world. The Canadian view toward Iran is also conflicting, I can say that there is no Iranian embassy here in this country. It got removed by previous Canadian Prime Minister Stephen Harper. Anyway, as an Iranian, if I want to get a passport here in Canada, I must contact the Pakistani embassy in Washington, because you guessed it, there is also no Iranian embassy in the United States of America. Before the Iranian Revolution in 1979, Iranians could travel to almost every country in the world, visa-free. Iran was almost as developed as all other Western countries, women were free, and Iran was a much-visited country. Look at us now, we've regressed, yet again here I am on the same topic I was on a few days ago. Today, Iranians can barely visit any country without a visa, and it simply is saddening. Can you see that just by talking about passports and travelling of all things, what the state of this country has now become? It is heartbreaking, Iranians do not even have the luxury of travelling freely. In fact, they do not have the luxury of anything.

My mother has got COVID-19 today, which is very sad to see, she is currently knocked out cold on the bed screaming my name every ten seconds. The coronavirus has many political views around it, I have a lot to say about it. To start, the Western world has dealt with this virus terribly, it has been here for around two whole years, and it is still in people's life. Of course, I am not expecting it to leave easily, but if we compare it to some places in the world, it seems as if they got rid of the virus and life is almost back to normal. My second view on this virus is a thought I have had for the past few days, where are all these variants coming from? Some have conspiracy theories; some believe it is natural and some believe it is due to science. Whatever it may be, I am sick and tired of seeing and hearing about COVID-19 everywhere I go. I just want to live my life normally. I must accept that this virus will never properly get rid of because it is a hard thing to do. Nevertheless, here is my little rant on this, and would I have ranted if my mother never caught the virus? Probably not. Things happen for a reason, and I am sure she will be fine, and I hope I now never have to talk about this subject ever again. Iran is also a country that has dealt terribly with the virus; however, I would not want to entirely blame it all on the government. They do not trust American vaccines or anything that is imported from the West. I must say however, that is what happens when you have zero diplomatic relations with, arguably the biggest powerhouse in the world today. I think that Iran should improve diplomatic relations with the West.

Of course, it will never happen under the IR, who believes everything that the West touches is poisonous, but when it comes to a matter like this, I think there should be some sort of deal because the lives of the people are at stake. But remember what I said at the beginning of this book, this regime does not care about the people. They only care about themselves. I would not even be surprised if every member of the IR government and its officials have taken American vaccines to save themselves. Nevertheless, it doesn't change the fact that the Islamic Republic has taken decisions that have, unfortunately, taken many of the Iranian people's lives. If I had never mentioned that we are talking about Iran, you, the reader, would assume that I am mentioning an underdeveloped country. That is yet another example of how Iran has regressed over the years. We cannot even take care of ourselves when there is a worldwide pandemic.

Instead of importing vaccines, the Iranian government decided to take matters into their own hands and fabricate their "own" vaccines.[4] They think it is that simple. This shows the incompetency of this regime, it is genuinely run by brainless people, you'll excuse me for my language.

I can stand here and complain about the Islamic Republic for days and weeks and months, but how can one change this country? For me, the answer is simple, Iran must be subject to a regime change. For that to happen, there must be a new revolution. A smart one this time, one that is more powerful than the 1979 Iranian Revolution. The Iranian people must revolt against this evil regime. How? Get to the streets! Unfortunately, that is a challenge. I would love to go for a quiet protest like what Mahatma Gandhi did for India and their independence. But that is nearly impossible because the Iranian regime would simply not budge. I am heavily against violence, but I am afraid that it will need to be present in a new Iranian Revolution. The brave Iranian people must go to the streets and burn the current flag of the country, which does not represent us in any way shape or form. We need to burn down the regime's posters, art and everything that is regime related within the country. These thieves have no place in a heavenly country just like Iran. It will take a long time before there will be any sort of reaction from the government, but I can guarantee you that there will be one, the brave people of Iran must keep fighting until the end. We will win at the end, whether it is tomorrow, in two months, in seven years or twenty years. We will win. I can assure you. The downfall of the Islamic Republic of Iran is a process that will take some time, we are sick and tired of this era. We, the youth of Iran are the new generation, and I can assure you that we will make sure the Islamic Republic is no more. The youth will not allow the IR to stay in power.

What I want the most for Iran now is a fair democracy. Not the "fair "democracy we are seeing around the world. We all know that is not an accurate representation of a "fair" democracy. My father and I have always been inspired by Iran's 35th Prime Minister, Mohammad Mossadegh who was overthrown in a coup d'état in 1953.[5] I understand many people are not too fond of him and believed in other people, which I find to be completely fine. Many people do not necessarily agree with his ideologies. My inspiration comes from his vision of a free and democratic Iran. This is a case where I want to fight for a free Iran. Mossadegh is one of many who envisioned such a feat. He volunteered for his service. He did not even have a salary as a Prime Minister[5]. He had so much commitment to fight for what he believed was right and for that, I do not believe that anyone can disregard his dedication and courage. He had endured so much, and for that, he will always stay a key figure in Iranian history. I hope to one day, be as influential as him. The only exception is that he, unfortunately, did not manage to fully fulfill his plans and dreams regarding a democratic Iran. Instead, he was arrested in 1953 following that coup d'état orchestrated by the UK and the USA. The Shah was then reinstated in power, and Mossadegh's government was dissolved. I believe that this situation shows how feared he was. I believe that the US and UK governments feared Mossadegh.

They felt threatened. In some way, the birth of the Islamic Republic of Iran is partly due to this case. I believe that both countries must apologize and acknowledge the harm that they have caused to Iranian politics.

Of course, there are people in this world that believe that the Islamic Republic is a good idea. It is perhaps very surprising, but we live in a world where everything can happen.

To that, I have a few things to say. For starters, look around you, look at how every other Asian country is evolving. Was Iran not once a prestigious powerhouse? Look at us now, we are clearly regressing. We have simply built a very bad image for ourselves. We went from being one of the best countries in the world to one of the worst.

It is fully within your right to believe in the IR's ideology, of course. But think about it, do you truly believe that what the Islamic Republic is doing today is good for the people? Do you not think that the IR's ideology is simply fueled by a battle of egos against the Western world, and not what is genuinely good for the people? This is what I think. Barely anyone is in favor of the IR now, and if you do believe in it. Change. That is really what I can tell you. The youth are against it, the women are against it and now most men are against it. The ideology of the IR has pushed us back for hundreds of years and it will continue to do so. We will not be able to persevere in anything. We will lose what we now barely have. The future of our country is not looking good. It has not looked good since 1979 and it will not look good for the next decades to come.

What a turn of events. As I am currently writing this, the United States of America is threatening Russia. According to them, a single additional Russian force entering Ukraine would trigger a US response.

These are exactly threats that can trigger world wars. Can this be the start of a new war in the world? Let's hope nothing happens. But we are talking about Russia and the US, two massive powerhouses in the world. Anything can truly happen. This ongoing Russia-Ukraine situation is something that has always intrigued me because in some way it resembles the Iran-Iraq war that happened a long time ago, way before I was born. Of course, they are not fully for the same purpose, but they are both neighboring countries going against each other. To be completely honest, after the COVID-19 pandemic, this is the last thing the world needed. If there is one thing I know about Vladimir Putin, the president of Russia, is that he is a man that is never willing to give up, no matter what the outcome is. He is a very scary man; indeed, therefore I am worried about this situation right now. Russia plans to invade Ukraine. I hope I do not get to wake up in the next few days to the news that Russia is sending its troops to Ukraine. Just give the world a few months of peace, please. I will start researching more on this matter because I do not know entirely everything about the feud between Ukraine and Russia. I always knew there was something wrong, but I never thought that it might come to this.

I will leave it at that for today.

After researching more about the ongoing Ukraine-Russia conflict and America's involvement, it makes me dislike America's politics even more. Its politics just loves putting its nose everywhere, even when they are not involved. That is the product of imperialism. The United States of America is imperialist. What saddens me the most about it is that people, most of them are completely oblivious to that fact. I have always thought of the United States as a self-interested country, a country that always claims to care for the people, but it is not. They lie too much, and I feel like in recent times most people got to see that side of them. To clarify, I do not hate Americans, I have nothing against the people of America. Americans can be friendly, and it is such a shame to see politics divide both the people of America and the people of Iran. Although, in Iran, I am sure that Iranians themselves have no problem with the people of America, despite what the Iranian government is trying to feed them in the media. Hopefully one day, we get to see both nations become friends again, not having to think what one country thinks about the other. Back to my original point, to combat the government of the United States is not so easy, they are the most powerful nation on Earth. I do not believe that they can be defeated. I think that the only way something big happens to America is if it happens from within. The country was in turmoil after the death of George Floyd for example. I had never seen America like that, and I was shocked. There were the capitol riots that also happened, nevertheless, recent times in America have not been so great.

Let's be honest with ourselves, despite all that, it is not enough to necessarily change the country. And why would you when your country is the biggest powerhouse in the world?

There is one person whom my father taught me to admire, and that is the great Noam Chomsky. He believes that America is "a leading terror state".[6] This is coming from an interview from many years ago. I have an opinion on that which I would like to share with all. I believe that some parts of the world are fed this narrative that mostly everything American-related is phenomenally wonderful and that it is a perfect world over there. That narrative is also very false. America is doing many things wrong. For me, it stems from the end of the Cold War when they seemingly went from a superpower to a hyperpower. The issue with this is that America could have been able to use this for the greater good, but instead they have decided to use it all for themselves which I do not blame them for. I am sure the same would've occurred with any other country around the world, including Iran. I fear America has gone too far, as previously stated above, they have their noses into everything that is going around the world. Is that not absurd? Let's face it, most problems post-Cold War arises from the United States of America, like it or not. What breaks my heart is that there are so many innocent people who have sadly passed away due to these many conflicts. I am thinking of many innocent Iraqis and Afghans who have ultimately done nothing to receive such a depressing fate. It will not stop any time soon, this is something that will go on for years, and maybe even decades. However, I will not stand here and say America does all these terrible things because Iran does the same. Unfortunately, this is where our world is now.

Enough talk about the United States, let's shift our focus back to Iran. So how do we exactly reform this damned Iranian government? Should it be another revolution? Or perhaps a coup d'état? It is hard to tell but I will attempt my best to explain my opinion on this because it is a hard question to answer. If you want a simple answer, whatever it takes to get rid of this regime is fine by me. If you want a more detailed answer, I firmly believe that a new revolution should take place. This time, a revolution from within and from without. The problem with this is that it will take a lot of time, from years to possibly even decades, who knows. But Iranian people have grit and determination, and if the effort is there, I am sure that it will be done.

Of course, running a revolution in Iran requires a lot, sadly we will have to sacrifice a lot for it too. It also requires the people's will, which I am sure is plenty. We, as people of the dear land of Iran, are and will always be stronger than the elites up top. Iranians worldwide will have to participate. Just thinking about it makes me smile. I would do anything for that to happen. Right now, Iranians need hope, will and belief if they want this to truly happen. We are a nation that has gone through a revolution, and you can bet we will do it yet once more. Hopefully this time, it will be the last time that we will have to put ourselves into such trouble. We all need to be smart with our decisions; I strictly do not want another repeat of the current regime this time.

Right, I may be about to say something a little bit controversial here. There is one thing that I agree with concerning the foreign policy of the Islamic Republic of Iran. Do not panic, let me explain myself. For many years now, we've constantly seen a battle between Israel and Iran. I have a dislike towards Israel's government, not the people, but the government. Again, like Iran, the people of both countries are often the victims. I do not agree with Israel's government and their sets of ideologies. I believe that they are a bunch of criminals. They have committed inhumane acts toward the poor people of Palestine. It is heartbreaking because they always manage to get away with it. We hear it all over social media, but never in the media. I have another wish, and that is that Palestinians and Israelis both manage to live in peace one day. Unfortunately, the Israeli government is so right-wing that I heavily doubt living in peace will ever happen. The Israeli government has done so much harm and, in my opinion, they are hypocrites too. I cannot believe they dare to blame Iran for things they also do. They are thieves and they have stolen the lives of thousands of innocent people who, yet again, I will keep saying, have ultimately done nothing to deserve such a tragic fate.

I will leave it at that for today, speaking about Israel's government always manages to put me in a bad mood. They can be so much better. It is a real shame.

It does baffle me to see Israel's government constantly get away with such inhumane activities. This is a matter that the whole world should acknowledge. Many of them do already, but more should. I believe that their activities are purely malicious, illegal even. These activities are backed by terrorists and funded by terrorists. Unfortunately, it seems to me like the United States of America and Israel are both countries that have built this notion of alliance where they can pretty much obtain whatever they please with absolutely no consequences. It becomes such a fuss when there is a matter that does not go their way, they are always the first to point fingers at others when often, they are the ones to blame.

We live in an era where politics seems to be all about ego as if they want to force a narrative that they probably know isn't the best idea, but they keep pushing it to prove rivals wrong. Perhaps I am wrong, but sometimes, these people cannot possibly think that what they are doing makes any sense. To add to that, people are too afraid to stand up in my opinion. It is a must; people must stop hiding and start speaking their thoughts and minds. Governments cannot suppress the people, there is no such thing. If people want something, they will eventually get it, but they will need to fight for it, however. That is the mentality I am giving myself to get rid of the Islamic Republic. That is the mentality that every Iranian should adopt if they want to also get rid of the IR. The government wants us to be afraid and defying that is the first step toward a revolution.

I also want to shed light on one other country, that I believe comes into play with Iranian geopolitics. That country is Saudi Arabia. Unfortunately, there is a current proxy conflict going on between both Iran and Saudi Arabia. For me, it seems like Saudi Arabia is looking to increase their influence in the Middle East. To do so, putting Iran down is a must, I also heavily believe that one of the reasons why Saudi Arabia and the United States of America are both allied, is exactly that, to put Iran down. If it is the case, I think this is a somewhat huge betrayal on Saudi Arabia's part. To explain this, I strongly believe that both Iran and Saudi Arabia should never even be feuding with each other. Both are close to being neighbors, and they are both technically Muslim countries. Growing up, I have had to learn the hard way that there is somewhat of a divide in Muslim society between Shia Muslims and Sunni Muslims, which I find, very unfortunate.[7] It should not matter if one is Shia or Sunni, at the end of the day, religion is one. Religion is made to bring people closer, not divide them. In this sacred world, everything is possible. I have always had this theory on what the world would look like if Saudi Arabia and Iran were allied together versus the Americans. It begs the question, is there something that Saudi Arabia is hiding from the world? Surely, a country that firmly believes in Islam cannot permit itself to side with the United States of America. I find that perhaps, something is up behind the scenes and soon I hope it will be discovered.

One opposition group that I always wanted to call out is the MEK, also known as the People's Mojahedin Organization of Iran. They are a radical political group, that was a key part in overthrowing the Shah in 1979, during the Iranian Revolution. [8] Funnily enough, now they are completely against the Islamic Republic, and they are advocating bringing their government into power.[8] Let me give you my understanding of the MEK. They are very hated in Iran, and I believe that the MEK should even be considered a terrorist group. You might now ask yourself why? Are they not against the evil regime of Iran? The answer to that is both yes and no. I believe that the People's Mojahedin Organization of Iran is not only anti-IR but also anti-Iran. Let me explain myself. I believe that their group is backed by people such as Mike Pompeo, the former secretary of state who served under Donald Trump when he was president. The group was also backed by people such as John Bolton and other highly respected people from the Trump administration.[9] Is that a coincidence? I think not. In addition to that, the MEK is a group that backed Saddam Hussein in the 1980s during the Iran-Iraq war.[9] What type of group goes against its own country and then claims that it is the right idea? It is ridiculous that people believe so. I also heavily believe that the group is funded by Saudi Arabia, although they have always rejected it, who else would be funding such money for them? I ask you yet again, dear reader. Is the MEK anti-regime like they claim they are or are they simply anti-Iran?

When Donald Trump was in office, I always had the impression that he had puppets around him. People who always agreed with everything he said or did. It sickens me. How can people like that even be in office? Mike Pompeo, the former secretary of state, is the one that keeps coming to my mind. In my opinion, he is an example of a person that only knows how to taunt people. I dare you, dear reader, to go listen to an interview of him. Notice how arrogant of a man he is. For sure, he does it on purpose. He wants to show that the United States is a dominant country. If you are smart, you would notice that his words are full of lies and nonsense. For me, Mike Pompeo is nothing less than a hypocrite and a liar. I would go to extreme lengths and even call him a terrorist myself.

Many of Trump's administration are people that have managed to get away with violations and crimes for which they will never get held accountable. For me, helping the MEK is one example. US politics sadly is just a bunch of scandals all piled up together and what is even sadder is that the people that are involved in it always somehow manage to get away with it. It seems like there is just no way of stopping it either. These people are no different from the people who run the Islamic Republic. Yet again, self-interest is key here. These thieves have one thing in common, they only do everything for themselves, not for the people.

Of course, all countries have "politicians" that commit scandals. But what happens in America particularly sparks an interest in me. How can a country that is known to be generally terrible with politics permit itself to try and rule the world by their means? It blows my mind. At the end of the day, I believe that giving the world to the hands of the United States would be a foolish move.

And that is why, in my opinion, the MEK is such a shame to the country and the people of Iran. They are supporting a state that will come to betray the country and its people the literal second they get the chance to. Therefore, I am insisting on boycotting the MEK, they are not a group that benefits the country and the people of Iran whatsoever.

Instead of attempting to make the country great again by their means, they have decided to ally with the Americans, which in my opinion, is not how they should do it. It is not good behavior, and, in my opinion, it is even a sign of betrayal. Again, the People's Mojahedin Organization of Iran are not anti-regime, they are anti-Iran.

Their ideology is clearly out of hatred and as stated above, it does not help the country it makes it worse. I hope their ideology doesn't go far. It is not a fair democracy and instead an easy route for both Saudi Arabia and the United States to do whatever they please with Iran.

Down with the People's Mojahedin Organization of Iran!

As stated in previous pages, the Iranian government vows revenge for the assassination of Qasem Soleimani.[1] I am bringing this issue back because I want to link the statement above with non-other than Donald Trump. In my personal view, I believe that Donald Trump is one of the few reasons for Iran's aggressive behavior. As I have mentioned many times before, politics is a battle of egos and both parties do not think about the citizens, therefore, I fear the worst for both societies. Both populations are fed a false narrative about each other that will just create even more hatred and maybe even violence. In my opinion, if America wants anything to do with Iran, I truly believe that a regime change must occur. Yet again I do not think America wants a regime change in Iran as it would not be beneficial for them whatsoever. Although Rudy Giuliani and Mike Pompeo, both working for the Trump administration have already advocated for one, they have done so in a completely wrong way. Pompeo thinks that a bombing campaign is necessary for a regime change.[10] A bombing campaign in Iran would be disastrous for Iran. But in my view, there is a reason why these two are advocating for such a terrible idea. If the United States of America successfully launches a bombing campaign, it will hurt Iran much more because it will be at its most vulnerable. That is exactly what the American government wants. They want Iran to be in a vulnerable position. If Iran ever reaches that position, the United States can then do what they please with the country, in some way, it will resemble what they have done to Afghanistan.

I can see right through you, Mike Pompeo. In my opinion, these thieves do not care about the Iranian people, they simply do not care about peace in the Middle East. What they want is what benefits them the most, and a bombing campaign would do exactly that.

But about now? Enough about Trump and his administration, they are currently not in power anymore. The current President of the United States is Joe Biden. What options does he have regarding Iran? What can the president of the USA do against an intransigent country that simply refuses to "play the rules of the game"? In my opinion, Biden has two options. The first one would be to work with the Islamic Republic and empathize with them to put them down afterwards. I believe that is not the smart move. What I want is for him to seek a regime change in Iran. If he doesn't, then he will be just as useless as the last few presidents of America because the truth is, all these conferences and useless talks have not led to anything in years. In my opinion, Joe Biden could help in a regime change to help the people of Iran, unfortunately, I do not think that will happen. Biden's plan when elected, was to rejoin the Iranian nuclear deal.[11] He believed that Trump failed to win the support of any US ally.[11] At this moment in time, the United States has not been able to revive the nuclear deal that Donald Trump successfully retreated from. It begs the question of whether it will ever be able to thrive or is just too late. A lot has been done to Iran during Trump's reign; he instated a travel ban which did not let any Iranian enter the country.[12] Which in my opinion, is a racist thing to do. I believe that the travel ban was simply made to discriminate against the Muslim countries that were banned, including Iran. Biden has since removed that disgraceful travel ban, which allowed many families to rejoice together.

I want to raise awareness of a tragic event that happened. An event that will be able to show you, the reader just how evil this regime is. A week ago, a poor innocent girl by the name of Mona Heydari was found beheaded by her husband in an act of "honor killing".[13] The husband was walking with her head in the streets of Iran. I believe that the Islamic Republic and the Sharia laws do not protect women's rights within the country. This is simply wrong. This "honor killing" has now sent alarming signals to other girls like her. That is also heartbreaking to know.

I want to fight for women's rights in Iran, and the world cannot just sit in silence while these poor women are suffering. I simply refuse to. I will do anything for the voices of women to be heard in Iran. It breaks my heart to see these atrocities that are still going on in Iran because an issue like that today is unacceptable and must be removed at all costs. In my opinion, Iran's misogynistic laws are also to blame but who truly is responsible for it all, is, of course, the Iranian regime that is adopting these laws. Remember when I said Iran is regressing? You would expect to see a story like this during the Roman Empire era, yet here we are, in 2022. Moreover, I am equally disappointed because there has been no statement from the United Nations. Where are they?

The truth is that Mona's life has been stolen. There is no honor in "honor killing", Mr. Khamenei.

Honor killing also does exist in other countries, and unfortunately, women and girls are the victims of such horrific actions.[14] In Iran, I believe that the government does not care about women, I view them as a misogynistic regime, as I have mentioned numerous times. They are the sole reason why Iranian women cannot thrive within the country. Let me give you an example, women in Iran, just like Mona and just like Sahar Khodayari are often in the news for being oppressed or killed. Have you ever seen an Iranian woman in the news for something positive? Very unlikely is the answer. The Islamic Republic has nullified women's rights in the country, and you possibly cannot advance as a country in this situation. And yet, here I am providing another example as to why Iran has regressed, it is a country that has so many bright girls and women, yet the IR have made them practically useless in Iranian society. On top of that, they even dare kill them. In Islam, the Sharia law is a law that is derived from the Qur'an. It is said that men must provide for their wives and their families which, if practiced normally should not be much of a problem. However, the Iranian regime has managed to twist the Sharia law. They made it into a law that heavily favors men for their benefit. I believe that women and men are equal. Having this twisted law in Iran means that you are treating women and young girls as second-class citizens. I ask again, how can Iran evolve as a nation when women's rights are completely neglected?

I have seen organizations around the world try their best to pressure the government, but over the years there has never been any real result from that. The United Nations has allowed this terrorizing regime to join the women's panel.[15] It is an absolute disgrace, coming from an organization that should be protecting women. The United Nations must also be blamed for a part of this and condemned for being silent on such horrific actions.

I want Iranian women to be able to lead the new revolution, I believe it is only right for them to do so. However, I must admit, doing that must be frightening. I am sure that the sacrifice will be worth it. Surely, with enough international attention, the regime will crack. For starters, I believe that the United Nations should remove Iran from the women's rights panel because I see that as a slap to the face of Iranian women. Then, with the United Nations by our side, perhaps the regime will finally take notice that people are slowly starting to realize their filthy tricks.

It will be so beautiful to see Iranian women lead a new revolution, I wonder what chants they will shout, and what actions they will take. They will finally be able to show what they have been holding in for all these years to the eyes of the public and it will be something very special to see. Frankly, they are the ones who deserve to be leading such an event, I believe that Iranian women are the biggest victims of the Islamic Republic ever since it came to power in 1979. They have had enough, and I am sure they will be the ones that will lead the next revolution in Iran.

Let's pave our attention to political prisoners in Iran, another batch of victims of the Islamic Republic. These political prisoners can range from women to men that have been forcefully sent to prison for simply expressing their opinions. In Iran, I believe that there is no freedom of speech. When I think of political prisoners, I think about the Iranian government committing some sort of genocide. Let me explain why. It is a genocide that has completely gone under the radar, and it is a subject that is barely talked about, in my opinion.

There is an estimate of around thirty-thousand political prisoners possibly executed.[16] However, I believe that the number is much lower than that. This is an issue that the regime has been trying to erase for the past forty or so years. This isn't something that they should get away with. Instead, this is an issue for which the regime should get condemned at the highest order. For sure, this issue is still ongoing. Narges Mohammadi, a very active political activist got arrested a few months ago.[17] I fear for her health, and I hope nothing bad happens to her. Some prisoners were peaceful against the regime but unfortunately, that is enough of a reason for the IR to ship them all to prison and make them suffer. These people are ordinary people, like you and me. They can range from professors to writers all demanding a free and fair Iran.

This cannot continue. Change.

Over the past few weeks, there has been another issue that has arisen in the country. I have a couple of thoughts and opinions about it. Teacher strikes are increasing. I believe that teachers do not get paid enough in Iran. These are people that wake up every morning in the hopes of providing the only education that the younger generation of Iran can have. These brave teachers must teach students that rights are worth fighting for. I understand that in a censored country like Iran, doing so is not so easy. When I was writing about political prisoners a few days ago, I mentioned that most often the victims are teachers who know much more than the elites. These people are simply trying to pass on their knowledge to the youth. But instead, they are sent to prison, and they are heavily censored. Regardless, I believe that low pay is a tactic from the Iranian regime to discourage these teachers, so they will not be able to do their jobs correctly. I hope these strikes and protests can lead to something bigger, and this can give people a chance who are tired of the IR, to go out in the streets and start a revolution. After all, any reason would do to go out and protest. I must admit, I do want the teachers to protest as much as they can and expose what is wrong in Iranian education currently and maybe even beyond that. I would hate for the regime to take advantage of these intellectuals and steal their yet again much-deserved pay for themselves and their associates. This is a reality in Iran, the government steals money from their people, and the teacher strikes are an accurate example of that.

What a turn of events, I cannot believe I am even writing this right now. Russia is invading Ukraine and I am sitting here thinking that there is no way there will be a war, all countries involved cannot have that reaction already, I have so many questions right now, I am slightly worried.

Is this a sign that the US dominance is coming to an end? Will Iran be involved in this? Does this benefit Iran or not? Like a chess game, we shall wait and see.

The United States and Israel are condemning Russia for breaching international law. [18] I find this particularly ironic since both Israel and the United States commit these horrors. What also sparks my curiosity is that there is no such sympathy for countries like Iran, Palestine, Libya, Iraq and much more, just like there is for Ukraine now. Do not get me wrong, the Ukrainian people do need much support and all the sympathy they get can get, but it all shows how easy it is for the West to manipulate the media. This conflict is all over social media now and all I see is one side of the story, which is the Western story. I believe that with all the sympathy being thrown around everywhere, people around the world are finally noticing how much the West is hypocritical, and I am glad that people are finally realizing this. I must admit, however, I believe it took them long enough. Let's hope that everything will be resolved in the upcoming days, I sincerely hope that there will be nothing major.

What a great start to the year…

It has been a few days since Russia invaded Ukraine and I have noticed many things, which I would like to share with you all. For starters, I believe that this conflict has exposed the double standards regarding how a country is portrayed and why. Although, I must admit that it is heartwarming that the whole world is standing with Ukraine. I would like to see that same love toward other countries that are not doing too well. Most specifically, Middle Eastern countries. I believe that this is due to social media. People are too dependent on that and with social media, you can never truly know the full picture.

Another entity to blame is news outlets, I believe that they are slowly getting outdated and unreliable, and they cannot be trusted much anymore. In this Russia-Ukraine conflict, I believe that everyone is trying to get on a side. The long-time battle between both Russia and the United States has hit Russia's neighbors. I believe that because of this battle, the Ukrainian people are the real losers of all. They are paying the price at the expense of pleasing evil political leaders who hate each other.

War is never the solution to anything, but for now, I am curious to see what Iran's plans are, I am very sure that they will claim to be neutral but secretly help Russia.

We will have to wait and see.

FIFA and UEFA have banned Russia from competing in international football.[19] I believe that this ban is not fair. It seems that politics have reached the realm of sports. Moreover, I want to call out both FIFA and UEFA for making a statement explaining to keep politics out of sports.[20] How can both organizations ban Russia for violating human rights, which has to do with politics and yet claim to keep politics out of the sport? I believe that it makes no sense, and that phrase must be changed. FIFA and UEFA get to decide what to keep in and what to keep out, in my opinion. With this same logic, countries like the United States, Israel, Saudi Arabia and even my own country, Iran, should be banned from football. These countries have all violated human rights, have they not?

The 2022 FIFA World Cup is also taken place in Qatar, it is now well known that thousands of migrant workers are sadly enslaved to work and make everything ready on time.[21] I believe that FIFA doesn't stand by its policies. They try to maintain this good image by using the sport of football as a shield meanwhile monstrosities are happening behind the scenes, like the poor migrant workers in Qatar. Now that we have established FIFA and UEFA's true intentions, I believe both organizations do not mind what is going on in Ukraine, rather they are using this to please everyone as if they are following a trend.

Over the past few days, I have seen numerous companies around the world removing everything that is Russian-related. I find that particularly captivating because just like UEFA and FIFA, I believe that they are not doing this to directly support Ukraine. They are rather doing it for media attention and as I stated yesterday, it is similar to following a trend. Where were these companies when thousands of Palestinians were dying on the street every day? They were nowhere to be seen. It infuriates me. I mentioned that there are double standards for this conflict, here is just another example. If these companies truly cared, they would remove products from most countries that have committed these acts. Unfortunately, life is like this. People hop on one side and defend it without even properly thinking. In some way, I also do feel for the Russian people, I believe that they are getting tons of hate and sadly all of it is due to the government's actions. It is unfair when you think about it, Russians and Ukrainians should be brothers and sisters, not rivals. We live in such a dark world where these thoughts should never be a reality, and sadly we wake up to see that it is. For now, I believe that this conflict will now go on for quite a bit of time, my hope that it would end quite soon has been put to an end. This conflict may take months or even years.

Let's hope I am wrong and that everything will come back into order in the near future.

I wonder what Iran's leaders are currently thinking about the Russia-Ukraine crisis. As I mentioned previously, I believe that Iran's government will claim to be neutral because on one hand, siding with Russia means that the whole world will be against us both. But on the other hand, Iran obviously will not side with the Americans. Iran's government will secretly help Russia in the war by supplying them with some military firepower if I were to guess. This Ukraine-Russia conflict might be beneficial for Iran's government after all, as I believe it will give them more time for the nuclear deal debacle. The nuclear deal has gone under the radar ever since this conflict started. As of now, I am curious to see if Russia will receive an abnormal number of sanctions for all of this. Iran is also a country that is heavily sanctioned which has badly affected our economy. Can something similar happen to Russia? It is a question that can only be answered with time.

In the meantime, however, I believe that people of color in Ukraine are not being properly treated. Most of them are being denied at evacuation points and most of them cannot even leave the country.[22] Unfortunately, it seems that this is poorly covered in the media when it should not be. I believe that this is yet another example of how the West can manipulate the media. Those people are stuck in the middle of a conflict with which they have nothing to do with.

It is official, Russia is now the most sanctioned country in the world, I must admit, it is very impressive that it took Putin a few weeks to achieve that.[23] Now, Russia believes that the sanctions imposed on them will affect the Iran nuclear deal, and it will create problems.[24] At this point, I do not know whom to believe anymore, they are all feeding a different narrative. Whatever it may be, Iranian leaders are licking their lips right now. Perhaps this can be a new era for the Iran nuclear deal. I believe this can remove a fair bit of sanctions and we might be able to see the Iranian economy become slightly better. However, I do not have many hopes, after all, the Iranian economy is so poor that it would take a miracle to save it under this regime. It has been hit with so many sanctions that it hasn't been able to do anything economic-wise. In my opinion, the sanctions are not much of an issue to the Iranian regime, it directly affects the people, like always, the Iranian people are the ones to suffer, for no reason at all.

The Iranian economy is one topic that does scare me for the future, it faces significant challenges that need to be addressed, but I believe we are in a situation where it may be far too late. I do not believe that there is much potential for growth and development regarding the Iranian economy. It is getting worse and worse by the day, and it does not seem like the IR is competent enough to take care of this concerning issue.

World news is going from bad to worse. Iran has officially attacked the United States consulate in Erbil, Iraq.[25] I believe that this attack is due to this Iran and Israel proxy war. On one hand, there is the Iran nuclear deal at stake, and on the other, it feels like the people in charge of Iran simply do not mind the Russia-Ukraine issue. It is bizarre to me. I believe that America will only condemn Iran for its actions, however, I am the most intrigued about what Israel's response will be. I consider Israel as America's "puppets". I believe that they will wait on America's proper response before doing anything themselves. If America does not come up with an answer, then questions need to be asked. Does Joe Biden even care about Iran anymore? Is the Iranian nuclear deal even going to happen? I truly am looking for answers. This Russia-Ukraine conflict has taken the center of everything, it seems like the world is only focusing on that matter. Perhaps, that could be the reason why Iran hit an American base in Iraq in the first place. Who knows at this point?

I have so many questions to ask, I hope I will be able to answer them all in the future. I certainly do not hope for an American response. What if this leads to another assassination? Will this lead to further complications? Will this affect the Iranian nuclear deal?

Today, two prisoners in Iran have been released, one notably Nazanin Zaghari-Ratcliffe. Zaghari-Ratcliffe is a key figure. Her imprisonment has caused a massive uproar in the media. She has been held in Iran for around six years.[26] Why? The government of Iran claims that she has done many things that are "against" the regime.[26] The Islamic Republic of Iran condemned her for being a spy.[26] They have also condemned her for training Iranian journalists that live abroad, meaning that they will spread anti-IR propaganda outside of Iran.[26] I believe that this is a scary case for every Iranian that lives abroad, do we now have to travel to Iran with such worry? One thing is for sure, the moment this book is published, I will probably never be able to step foot in Iran, which is a sad thought. My opinions on Zaghari-Ratcliffe are mixed, on one hand, I do not think she has necessarily done anything wrong, but on the other hand, you never know, there will always be doubt. Nevertheless, it doesn't justify imprisoning her for six years and mistreating her, that is not fair. Iranian leaders do not know what being fair means, anyways. Sadly, I believe that if this regime stays in place, we will see more imprisonments just like in this case, and yet again, Iran will not advance as a country. Not only that, but this gives a terrible image to Iranians abroad who perhaps, some have never even gotten the chance to visit their homeland. Let's hope this regime falls because enough is enough. Every day there is news of tragedies regarding Iranian people. At one point, it really does need to stop.

It has been a few days since anything significant has happened regarding the Russia-Ukraine situation, so I want to shed light on just how racist the Western media can be. In recent weeks, Western media have often dragged the name of some Middle Eastern countries such as Iraq and Afghanistan and set them as an example for war.[27] I have called out the hypocrisy of the West numerous times throughout this book, but I believe that it is now time to call out some of the Western media for their racist remarks. I believe that they should be held accountable for such actions. You must understand, dear reader, that this media is the one that is feeding information to today's youth. It is heartbreaking to see that they are exposed to false information, or as Donald Trump likes to call it, fake news. This must change, I do not want the Western youth to grow up with an idea that the Middle East is not good. I do not want them to think of the Middle East as this war-torn part of the world. I believe that Western media is trying to portray this image that war never does happen in Europe but normally happens in the Middle East.

This must change, I am disappointed in Western media, but not surprised. People do not seem to care that much either, it further proves to me that we are heading in a direction where the Middle East will be set as an example for war. This should not be the case, as war can happen anywhere around the world.

As much as I do not condemn what Russia has done to Ukraine, I wonder what would happen if Ukraine did join NATO. NATO is an organization that "guarantees" the freedom and security of all its members.[28] Here is my take on this; Ukraine thinks that Russia invading them is wrong, and rightfully so. But what about joining NATO which means allying with the United States and non-NATO ally Israel, which in return has and will invade countries and territories? How can Ukraine be okay with that? That is what I think. Does it beg the question, is the Ukrainian government as innocent as the media is portraying them to be? I am not so sure. I believe that President Volodymyr Zelenskyy is being portrayed as an angel in the media.

After the Cold War, Russia was promised by the West that NATO will not expand further into the east.[29] This is an important claim, and it is key to understanding most of Putin's motives. Putin has called this issue and has accused the west of essentially breaking their promises and lying to them.[29] The Russia-Ukraine crisis can be compared to the 1962 Cuban Missile Crisis, which was a historical confrontation between the Soviet Union and the United States.[30] The Soviet Union wanted to install missiles in Cuba, to protect itself, as it cannot directly hit the US if an attack were to happen.[30] After negotiations, the Soviet Union withdrew what they installed in Cuba.[30] In 2022, the roles are reversed, the US is now the one who is expanding to the east nearby Russia. As I have said many times, politics is nothing more but a battle of egos, the Ukraine-Russia crisis is yet another example.

I had a conversation with my father regarding what the war will look like when it is done. We both believe that it all depends on how it ends and when it ends, for all we know, this can end in eight years, just like it could end within the next few days. The Russian economy is doing poorly now, the sanctions put in place have influenced the economy. I have seen throughout social media and news outlets that Russians are not doing too well themselves, which I take with a grain of salt. I believe that all of this is a way for the United States to create this narrative that Russia is weak and that they are losing the battle.

However, if Ukraine does join NATO, I believe not much will change, I think that the dominance of the United States will increase and they will continue what they do usually, oppressing nations and states that are not adequate to their sets of ideologies.

On the other hand, if Russia manages to pull off what they are doing, then the world of politics can turn upside down, and perhaps that can be the beginning of a new era for countries like Iran, North Korea, and China. It is scary to see that the world is in the hands of two of the world's biggest powerhouses and there is absolutely nothing anyone can do about it.

Let's shift our focus back to Iran and back to the prisoner that was released a few days ago, Nazanin Zaghari-Ratcliffe. What about the other prisoners that are left behind, what will happen to them? Should Iran stop detaining all these dual nationals? The answer is a resounding yes; both morally and ethically. We all know the Islamic Republic has blood on its hands. They cannot detain everyone that isn't fully Iranian. How can the Iranian regime make a good country with conditions like that? The regime is scaring its people away. In my view, the only two solutions to this would be either a deep reform or a regime change. This is not an issue that can be solved this easily, no matter what an individual does, if it is against the regime, they can get sent to prison. I understand that by detaining these people, the regime is trying to portray a message to the West that they are not a country to be "messed" with. I believe that this issue is hurting the country even more because all it shows to the West, is exactly what they are portraying in the media, that Iran is an evil country with no morals. There is some truth to that. Furthermore, I believe that nowadays, it simply isn't worth it to visit Iran. What is the point of going there if you have a good chance of getting captured and sent to prison for many years? There is so much more to this, in Iranian prisons, rape and sexual assault are used as a weapon.[31] This regime is barbaric, and these executions are showing how badly Iran has regressed as a country. Executions were a thing thousands of years ago.

However, for the Iranian regime, it seems that they are still a thing used to oppress and scare its citizens away.

When your country is run by such crooks and criminals, you can also expect your football national team to be affected by it. Today, Iran's national football team played against Lebanon's national football team for the 2022 FIFA World Cup qualifiers. It was said that Iranian women would be let in to watch the game.[32] Unfortunately, these women were greeted with pepper spray.[32] They have been sprayed with pepper spray for simply wanting to watch a football game. I have so many questions. For starters, why would the regime let Iranian women buy tickets for such an event in the first place? To give false hope? It doesn't make any sense. Iranian state television censored the event.[32] To top it all off, the Iranian football federation has claimed that women were never even meant to be attending the event.[32] I am waiting to see if FIFA will step in or if they will go on about their business, just like usual. I am sure there will be plenty of other football controversies down the line, and I will be documenting them. In truth, I believe that Iranian football has always been political. If you are an Iranian football fan like I am, you would understand how much of a struggle it has been to support this national football team.

In a few days from now, there will be the official draw for the World Cup, which is held in November. I am very excited, yet very nervous at the same time. Let's hope for some positive news.

Today was the official draw for the 2022 FIFA World Cup. Of course, politics will yet again play a part in this. Iran has been placed in the same group as England, either one of Ukraine, Scotland, or Wales and you guessed it, the United States of America. I wish I was joking. For context, Iran played a historical World Cup game against the USA, in 1998.[33] That also came with its own sets of problems. Iran won that game 2-1, and it is a game that is still talked about to this date.[33] Sadly, I was not alive when that game was aired live to the millions of people that were watching, worldwide. I can only imagine what the world will be like for this upcoming game. Iran is playing its geopolitical rival at the World Cup, is this an April Fool's joke? Of course, tensions were a lot worse in 1998 than it is now, and something completely different from back then compared to now will be the use of social media. The footballing world is already going crazy about this, and it hasn't even been a full day yet. I am expecting news outlets to profit from this as much as they can, and I do not necessarily blame them either. Having Iran, the United States of America and England in the same group is unheard of, and I am excited to see what happens in the future. I also do hope that these games bring both people together. In 1998, Iranian players were not allowed to shake hands with American players, instead, they brought out flowers and gifts.[33]

I hope these games bring the players and both nations together, in a world where hatred is common among all parties involved, it will be refreshing to see them shake hands for once.

I have always had a theory on how an Iranian revolution can occur, of course, it is easier said than done. But I have intensively studied the Tunisian Revolution and I believe that something similar can be done in Iran. Social media played a huge role in the Tunisian Revolution, it played a part in protest mobilization and emotional mobilization.[34] I believe that social media is one of the reasons that led to the Arab Spring and the downfall of Ben Ali's regime. Ben Ali was the president of Tunisia at that time.[34] The Internet is censored in Iran, and the Iranian regime is very good at manipulating Internet access within the country.[35] The question arises, can the Iranian people manage to do a similar thing in Iran? At first glance, perhaps not, but I think our voice should come from both within and outside of Iran itself. The mainstream media must help, although in my opinion that it is extremely unlikely. We, need to push it to the limit, as much as we can, at least enough for the world to see. In the past, we have seen glimpses of it, notably during the 2017 Iranian protests, where people were organizing protests and sharing videos online.[36] I believe that all we truly need is an extra push, but it does take the will of the people, such a feat will not be accomplished if no one is willing to help. Social media is very powerful, and it can make certain things possible, for once, I hope social media can be used for downing the Islamic Republic of Iran.

The question is, how do we start this? Of course, the best answer is to flood the streets as we have always done in the past. My deepest wish would be another case like the Green Movement, a movement that symbolized the removal of former Iranian president Mahmoud Ahmadinejad.[37] His opposition, Mir-Hossein Mousavi, was claimed to have gotten more votes than Ahmadinejad. The Iranian regime was accused of rigging the elections.[37] I believe they did so. This time around, however, a new movement in Iran should not have as a goal to remove the current Iranian president, but rather, remove the whole system of the Islamic Republic. Iranians protesting around the world should be a positive, perhaps that can get recognition and world leaders can do something for once, although I believe that is unlikely. Iran needs another version of Mousavi, who was a reformist that had many opposing views to the Islamic Republic, he actively supported women's rights and was open to negotiating with the West.[38] I admire this man; he has risked his life to defy the regime. Mir-Hossein Mousavi was placed under house arrest.[39] He gave Iranians, including a 12-year-old version of me, lots of hope. That is one thing Iranians have always, and will always have, and that is hope. I believe we Iranians can make history once again. The Green Movement in Iran helped galvanize a new generation of activists and civil society groups, it also has helped raise enormous international attention and important questions about the role of democracy and human rights in Iran's political system.

Now, we need to figure out which type of government would be the most beneficial for Iran. Ideally, I believe that a unitary government with a good functioning presidential system would be the best option to go for. I have heard some people in my surroundings offer an idea of a federal system, which I am not completely against, but I fail to see how that would work in Iran. The country is unified enough, we already have a true sense of identity that federalism offers. Yet I would not mind it because it would be better than what we currently have. Iran needs a unitary system. We need a president who will be able to take control of the country. Hopefully, sanctions will be minimized by then, and Iranians can start dreaming again. In terms of infrastructure and lifestyle, perhaps the country will resemble France and the countries nearby. Iran must be democratic, and it must be able to show a fair representation of democracy. As I am writing this, all this only looks like a dream, but one can believe and hope. Other than that, Iran needs to nationalize its banks and oil. I believe that oil is not in the hands of the people but rather in the hands of the regime, just like it also was during the Shah's era. Realistically, we need to take this step by step because it is nice to be able to discuss what a future Iran would look like, but if there is no action then there is no point in doing so. For now, the focus must always be to remove the evil regime in Iran.

Today, I have learnt that there have been various humiliating treatments regarding Afghan refugees in Iran. This is a case that should be called out and fixed by the United Nations in my opinion. There have been issues like this last year, where it was reported that thousands of Afghan refugees have been deported from Iran.[40] This upsets me, Afghanistan is a country that is very dear to us because they are our neighbors and to see that they cannot even enter the country that is next to them is truly heartbreaking. These people are coming to Iran to escape bloodshed and violence after the Taliban took over the country's capital, Kabul.[40] There is a humanitarian crisis in Afghanistan and its people need help, they cannot get it from Iran due to the incompetent regime that is in place. But the question yet again arises, why are Afghan refugees kicked out of Iran? Politically, it does not make much sense, Afghanistan is not allies of the West, so I believe that it cannot be due to that. However, I believe that the Islamic Republic thinks that with the many Afghan refugees entering the country, perhaps there will be a rise in unemployment for Iranians themselves. Nevertheless, this is still wrong. The IR claims that in Islam, everyone is equal, so why kick these poor people out, when all they are looking for is a second chance in life? It shatters my heart to see this unfold right in front of my own eyes. The people of Afghanistan have been terrorized enough over the years by the war regarding the United States of America, and now they must deal with the Taliban takeover. It is simply not fair for them.

These people need our help and instead of providing help, the Iranian government prefers terrorizing them even more.

Another day, another useless threat from Iran toward Israel. Today, Iranian president Ebrahim Raisi released a statement threatening Israel, telling them there will be complications if Zionists (referring to Israel) make the tiniest move that can threaten Iran's security.[41] We have seen these types of threats over a hundred times in the past and of course, there has been no action from both side every single time. Truth is, I believe that both regimes are quite the same, the only difference is that they believe in different beliefs. The reason why this threat has been public today is because of an attack from the Iranian military towards a site in northern Iraq, which Iranian officials believe that such site is used maliciously by Israel.[41] You see, these are cases that contribute to the Iran-Israel proxy war. They always go back and forth but, in my view, it seems like all of it leads to nothing. It compliments my original point where I mentioned that all of this is nothing more than just a battle of egos, there isn't much thought behind it either. The people are the ones that are suffering the most from it. This truly needs to stop. In some ways, I see both the Israeli and the Iranian officials as two very childish governments.

I will leave it at that for today, I cannot wait for this threat to yet again, lead to absolutely nothing. Watching both parties going back and forth is like watching two babies crying and screaming at each other.

A few days ago, there have been numerous clashes in the Al-Aqsa Mosque in East Jerusalem. I have explicitly waited a few days before giving my thoughts and opinions on the matter. Israeli forces raided the mosque and thus injured many Palestinians.[42] To the more mainstream world, this is an issue that you most likely have not heard about. Why? Because the Western media has barely covered the matter, although it is a big issue. I usually would like to compare the long feud between Palestine and Israel with the situation that is currently happening in Ukraine, with Russia invading them. I believe that Israel is responsible for invading Palestine, but what bothers me is how badly this issue is treated in the media. It is sickening that all you see in the news is how Russia is invading Ukraine repeatedly when the people supporting Ukraine such as Israel have been doing the same for years. It is immoral. We live in a society where it is easy for the police to get inside a mosque and start fighting with everyone. What have Palestinians ever done to deserve such a beating? All these people did that day, was wake up and go pray and that was enough to send some of them to the hospital, wounded and almost dead. Israel's government is a cruel regime and they do not have morals, exactly just like the Islamic Republic of Iran. Dear reader, do you not see a common pattern? I hope people reading this will open their eyes to the cruelty that this world offers, more specifically, the cruelty that the most important players of today's politics are committing.

I want to take a break from real-life news. Today, I had my International Relations final which I know I have done well. It consisted of an essay question which, in my view, is a very interesting one. My answer to this final is something I do not want to deprive the world of. I believe that my answer should be available to the world. The essay question was as follows: What do you think is the biggest threat the world is facing today? Of course, I had to use class material, or else my answer would've been seven words: the United States of America and Israel, and that would've been it. I answered with equality. My reasoning behind this was backed by a few Marxist theories and realist/neorealist views on global security. Another huge issue in our society is capitalism. Countries such as the United States seek more power and influence, rather than perfecting the world by being equal like they claim to be. To add to that, the world we live in is a brutal arena where states seek to achieve security at the expense of their neighbors. I have given numerous examples of such a statement in this book, there is the ongoing Russia and Ukraine crisis, and of course the Palestine and Israel conflict. In our lifetime, we will never be able to truly live in peace. I believe that permanent peace is something that will never be achieved, no matter how hard we fight for it. Therefore, the world is unequal. Because permanent peace does not exist in our society.

In an ideal world, permanent peace might exist, but on Earth, it is impossible.

Iran and Canada are scheduled to play a friendly football match in less than a month.[43] You would think that there is nothing wrong with that, but it has been all over Canadian news over the past few days. The controversy stems from an event that happened over two years ago. On January 8th, 2020, Ukrainian Airlines Flight 752 was shot down by the Iranian military.[43] Out of the 176 people who were on that flight, 55 of them were Canadian.[43] I can understand why some people would be opposed to this game, claiming that Iran should not step foot in Canada. On the other hand, if you understand football, you will perhaps understand why Canada Soccer planned to play Iran. They drew Morocco in their World Cup group, a team that Iran had previously played. I do feel compassion for the families and the tragic event. These people advocate cancelling the game, and I have mixed opinions on that statement. I do not think cancelling the game would do much to the regime and I think it would make things slightly worse. The mistake comes from Canada Soccer itself which should have not considered the game in the first place, but it is too late to cancel it. The Canadian football federation will most probably be subject to being fined if they do, and that means that the IR will get more money in their pockets. At the end of the day, is that the smart choice? I always grew up thinking of Team Melli, a nickname for the Iranian national football team, as the team of the people. Many Iranian football players have protested the government, notable players like Ali Daei, Masoud Shojaei and just now, Voria Ghafouri, are examples. Most players are against the regime but in a dictatorship like Iran, it is very hard to speak out against it, or your football career will seemingly come to an end. Therefore, I do not agree with people saying that the Iranian national team is the government's team, these poor players cannot do much or their lives will be at stake. This is all a mess, and I feel bad for both the Canadian and Iranian players who are being dragged into this matter.

Today, Canadian Prime Minister Justin Trudeau mentioned that a friendly between Canada and Iran is ill-advised.[44] Of course, he is subject to his own opinion, but who are you to say such a thing when Canada has no problem playing with countries like the United States, for example? I heavily believe there would be no problem playing a country like Israel too. That is what I think, but his word is much bigger than mines.

After many days of suspense, the Canada-Iran game has officially been cancelled.[45] It led to an uproar and a huge divide between fans of the national football team and the people who wanted this game to get cancelled. This is the last thing the Iranian people need, we do not need to get divided, this is certainly not the time, in my opinion. Iran's football federation will be looking to get some sort of compensation from the Canadian football federation.[45] This was something that I expected as soon as I heard rumours about the game getting cancelled. No matter what the amount will be, you can be sure that the money will not go to Iran's football federation but rather into the regime's back pocket. We can also be sure that they will go back to committing their atrocities, just like they have done for the past 40 years. The question arises, does this cancellation hurt the regime? Has the IR been weakened? Has the mixing of politics and sports led to anything in this situation? In my opinion, I do not think so. On the other hand, I think this has benefitted the regime, seeing that they will get their money for seemingly doing nothing.

To the dear viewer reading this, can you see throughout this book, that Iran is getting worse day by day? The world seriously needs to wake up.

There have been nationwide protests in Canada against the Iranian regime, set up by multiple groups. I assisted them. Two groups were protesting today, the MEK, and the worker's group. I was part of the worker's group because I do not agree with the views of the MEK, as mentioned previously. However, they were much better set up than us, they had multiple banners explaining their cause, with big images that were anti-IR related, I was impressed. A lot of effort was made. In our corner, we had a simple long banner that we all were raising Fortunately, our corner had a lot more coverage thus many pedestrians and journalists were taking videos and pictures of us. Everyone had masks to cover their faces in case Iranian officials stumble upon it. I was the only one without one because frankly, I am not scared of the regime. I want them to know that I will always be against them, no matter what. Another touch that was wholesome for me, is how both groups came together for the tragic events in Abadan. Last week, an unfinished building collapses in the region of Abadan, killing dozens of people.[46] This event led to protests both at the national and international levels, hence why I went to these protests today. People were not only denouncing the regime, but they were also denouncing how poor the construction is in this country and the cost of food prices, which were increasing for everyone.[46] I hope the world gets to see what is going on in Iran now, and perhaps something even bigger will occur.

I was not alone in those protests; I was with some members of my family. One member was in the corner of the MEK. I am fine with that; they have the right to support what they want. All my life, I have heard nothing but foul language regarding that group, I oppose them as mentioned previously. That does not mean that I do not want to hear their point of view, it piqued my curiosity. I wanted to see their perspective and know why they support such a group. The member of my family in question, which I will not reveal the identity of, told me things that I moderately agreed with, for example, he compared a garbage worker and a doctor, and he explained that both contribute the same in society, yet they are seen differently in society. They were explaining that MEK believed in equality.

However, the branch of the MEK that I heavily disagree about is how they work with the United States. I explained my view to them, and they replied to me that the reason why they are both allied is that our enemy is not the United States, but the IR itself. I disagreed. I believe that both are Iran's true enemies. One is as bad as the other, in my opinion.

How can the MEK permit itself to help the US, and say that they are in support of the Iranian people? Helping the United States is helping Israel, essentially, you are helping criminals.

So far, there have been numerous mass shootings in the United States, it is scary, to be honest. This time, the mass shooting occurred in Illinois. The shooter killed seven people during an Independence parade.[47] I want to shed light on this, simply because I believe that it seems that the United States is interested more in foreign policy than its own country. There have been numerous debates about whether guns should be allowed within the country but the issue that interests me the most is why can they permit themselves to meddle in issues that do not concern them yet have so many problems at home. I believe that the West is not a perfect world like they claim it to be. It has its problems, and this is one of them, particularly in the United States. It is demoralizing for an Iranian like me to see the West consistently drag Iran's name in a bad way when they are not doing so well themselves. It is surreal, I find that bizarre. But that is how Western media is, they are perfect and anyone else is below them. That is how it truly feels, in my experience. I must admit, all these mass shootings are absurd, why is the American government not doing something about it? I am sure that these mass shootings will keep increasing over the course of the year and it seems that it will just never stop, so many innocent people have passed away in that country.

It reminds me of a certain Islamic Republic…

Speaking of shootings, something very sad happened today. The former Prime Minister of Japan, Shinzo Abe, has been shot dead.[48] He was shot during a speech, in the neck.[48] The perpetrator intended that he did not agree with an organization in which he believed that Abe was involved.[49] Japan is not known for its gun violence, it has very strict gun laws. The perpetrator made a homemade handgun, which is impressive, yet tragic.[48] I want to shed light on this, although this has nothing to do with Iran and its politics, I do believe it is important for me to emphasize that this portrays a message to any current and future politicians. This shows that no matter where you are in the world, and no matter what you believe in, there will always be someone willing to take you down. In my case, the IR would be all over me if I ever stepped into Iran. The moment this book is published, I believe I will not be welcome in Iran anymore. Nevertheless, I believe that Japan is now terrorized, and this event will stay in people's minds for a very long time, maybe it will lead to new shootings. I hope not, but we've seen that happen in some places in the world, like the United States and such a feat is entirely possible.

Over the past few weeks, there is also another event that happened which I want to shed light on because I want to link it with what can happen to Iran in the future. The country of Sri Lanka is in a political and economic crisis.[50] This crisis caused the current Prime Minister, Gotabaya Rajapaksa, to flee the country to the Maldives.[50] He had promised to resign as the Prime Minister of the country, yet failed to do so.[50] One part that intrigues me, is how protestors from all parts of the country have stormed offices of the government to pressure them into stepping down.[50] It begs the question, why are Iranians not doing the same? The people of Sri Lanka have been struggling with fuel, food, medicine, and electricity.[50] I believe that Iran is also in a similar position. I believe that Iranians are also hit with some of these sets of issues, such as fuel problems and the cost of living. All these images that are coming out of Sri Lanka can and should be used as encouragement to the Iranian people to fight against the evil regime. Of course, storming offices and buildings in Iran is a lot more dangerous than in Sri Lanka, government officials and the military are much stronger in Iran than in Sri Lanka, but I believe that sacrifices must be made. As I have mentioned in the past, to be able to get past the murderous Islamic Republic, the people will have to pay a lot of sacrifices. But I believe it is all worth it. If Sri Lanka can succeed, I am well sure Iran can. With much hope and determination, the possibilities are endless. But we need to act fast before this regime becomes even more rotten than it currently is.

I hope the people of Sri Lanka get what they want, and may they obtain justice and peace.

Look at the date, look at it very closely. Today is the day that Queen Elizabeth II passed away.[51] She was Britain's longest-serving Queen, she served for seven decades.[51] This news does not have anything to do with Iran at all but even so, I believe that it is worth mentioning. It is never nice to discuss someone's death. I must admit however, I am not particularly a big fan of hers either. For the next few days, I am expecting millions of people around the world to mourn her death. What is unfortunate in my opinion is how no one will mourn the millions of people that have unfortunately died due to her calls and her beliefs. No one will talk about an issue this tragic. Therefore, I want to shed light on this situation. I believe that the British Empire has committed numerous atrocities. In addition to that, they should be held accountable for their history of colonization in many different places around the world. Why should I, as an individual, feel bad for such death when she has caused pain, suffering and years of distress to many populations around the world? It is not fair to the people who died because of the actions of the British Empire. In 1952, Kenya suffered, there were tons of detention camps, and stories of rape and castration.[52] It is a tragic situation; I believe many people are uninformed of her past. After all, these sorts of stories never get popular in the English media. Instead, I believe that the Queen is being treated as an angel, someone who has never done anything wrong. It is all false.

A few days ago, Iran's morality police arrested a 22-year-old female named Mahsa Amini.[53] She later died because of her injuries.[53] We can expect that it is due to the conduct of the said "morality police". The morality police in Iran patrols the streets of Iran to seek out people who do not adhere to the Islamic Republic dress code.[53] For the government, it seems that taking away someone's life is more important than a dress code. There have been numerous videos that were surfacing around the Internet and to be frank, it was hard to watch. It was disturbing and I could not watch the entirety of them. You need to have an inhumane government to see that people are killing each other over how they look. This woman has passed away for no reason and it sickens me, here is an example of another Iranian life that has been stolen.

In 2020, the supreme leader of Iran, Ali Khamenei, issued a speech about the murder of George Floyd, he condemned the United States by stating that the murder shows the real face of the American government.[54] It is shocking to see him state that because his government has been doing the same since they rose to power. I believe that the death of Mahsa Amini is a murder, the Iranian government has murdered her. It is pathetic that this is an issue ongoing today. I hope there will be more to follow, I hope this pushes the Iranian people to act. There have been protests for months and this should add fuel to the fire.

The past few days may have been the craziest days of Iranian politics we've had in the past few years, I would say. The death of Mahsa Amini has now caused a major uproar across the country and even across the world.[55] The president of Iran, Ebrahim Raisi flew to New York to discuss human rights, all while his own country is going nuts over numerous human rights violations.[56] Raisi cannot fool the whole world anymore; this is now a much bigger fight than it was a few days ago. My father went to New York to protest, and I wanted to go, but due to school and examinations, I could not. The world is slowly starting to take notice. The only worry I have now is how long all of this will last, but perhaps this can lead to much bigger things. One can only hope. I am expecting Iranian officials to start shutting the Internet and social media down, just like they always do when protests start erupting. But we are much stronger than that. I am glad to see the brave people of Iran standing up for Mahsa, I hope she, from above, is smiling at our actions now. There will be a lot more people that will get arrested and killed, but we must keep going right until the end.

Time is ticking and I hope this time the Islamic Republic of Iran will go down, once and for all.

Patience is key.

Once again, the worldwide protests regarding the death of Mahsa Amini are growing.[57] Today, these protests ranged from London to Tokyo to here, in Canada. The protests I went to were very big. I was surprised as to how many went out for them. We were around 10,000, quite possibly even more. It was empowering, I felt invincible. I felt like nothing in the world could stop us. People were chanting, crying, and screaming for this regime to go down. Emotional songs were being played; I could not help myself but cry. I let everything out, tears were flowing down my cheek, I have never felt so proud of my people. My mother was also crying; I could tell how much this meant to her. This is what freedom means to us Iranians. Our people have been robbed of basic human rights for years because this murderous regime is trying to take them away from us. We walked for hours until we stopped and started singing numerous famous freedom songs, reminiscing it right now is getting me emotional, believe me. I was happy to see the news outlets and social media finally covering our voices, for once. My friends were telling me about it, they cared about it, and it made me smile. This must go on until the regime falls, we cannot permit ourselves to stop at any given moment. I expect Iranians to be in a brutal battle with the regime in the next few days and months to come and I hope everything will go well. This might be the start of a new Iranian Revolution; this is our chance to shine and fight.

I believe that Khamenei, as usual, will blame the United States and Western ideology for all of this. But we Iranians are not falling into the same trap again, this time we are ready.

Justin Trudeau and the Canadian government are claiming that they are considering sanctioning the IRGC with new measures.[58] The IRGC is short for the Iranian Revolution Guard Corps, which in short is Iran's armed forces. I believe that is not enough. The government of Canada must at all costs, consider the IRGC as a terrorist group. Just like the United States does. But, for now, this is a step in the right direction. These new measures and sanctions now mean that thousands of IRGC-related members cannot step foot in Canada.[58] Canada is a top place for IRGC members to come and live here, far away from the chaos that is happening in Iran. They have their pockets filled with money stolen from the innocent people of Iran and it is heartbreaking to see them come here to settle, just as if nothing had happened. I also believe that this decision from the Canadian government was forced. In the past, they have never seemed to acknowledge the Iranian Revolutionary Corps as a big threat. Why now? After all these years of protests from Iranians in Canada, they are finally starting to hear our voices. I hope there will be better measures added in the future. Perhaps they are waiting for a better time to do so. Perhaps they are waiting for the Iranian regime to show cracks of stepping down.

I just hope the Canadian government does something; it would make thousands of Iranian Canadians very happy. Most of them have managed to flee the Islamic Republic, they did so to not have their lives stolen.

Iran is in complete turmoil now. Today, the famous Evin Prison was on fire.[59] Now, it is not clear what is going on, it begs multiple questions. Are the guards being attacked? Are the prisoners being attacked? Nobody knows and it is scaring me. However, this is reminding me of the Cinema Rex incident. In 1978, a cinema was set on fire, it killed around 400 people.[60] That event triggered the 1979 Iranian Revolution. Now, in 2022, I am asking myself the same. Will history repeat itself? Does this Evin Prison fire mean more than just what it is? Is this now the start of a new Iranian Revolution? I now believe that the prisoners are the ones that are being attacked in the prison. Evin is notoriously known for its political prisoners. Perhaps this is now an attempt for the Islamic Republic to brush off remaining political prisoners that currently are sentenced at that place. What is important to know is that amongst those political prisoners, there might be some that do come from foreign countries. If anything were to happen to them, perhaps this Evin Prison fire would lead to much more. Over the next few days, there will be more news and details on what has exactly happened at Evin. For now, I hope this will lead to much more, I want this to be a similar incident to the 1978 Cinema Rex fire, where it does lead to an Iranian revolution. Let's also hope nothing major happens in that prison, I hope no innocent political prisoners get hurt.

Death to the Dictator!

During these past few days, there have been numerous debates and opinions about whether the Iranian national football team should participate in the 2022 FIFA World Cup in Qatar. I have said it many times throughout this book, and I will say it again, there should not be the involvement of politics in sports. Ukraine wants to exclude Iran's spot at this World Cup.[61] It claims that Iran should not be at this World Cup, due to suspicions that the Iranian regime is supplying Russia with missiles during the Ukraine invasion.[61] Although they have all the right to be unhappy with the country of Iran, I still fail to see how that should be associated with the Iranian national football team, who have ultimately done nothing. I believe that banning Russia from football competitions was unjust and unfair to the players. It seems that now Ukraine will try to push to do the same for Iran. The World Cup starts in less than a month, however, I do believe that it seems very unlikely that Iran gets kicked out of the competition. With that being said, we have seen the unlikely with this national team in the past so I would not rule this possibility out. I do not want the Iranian national team to be banned from the World Cup, I believe that it is too late for that. I am expecting the Iranian national team to come forward and show support for the Mahsa Amini protests in due time but what scares me is the regime. I am sure they will have all of this under control. It will not be that easy for the players to pull it off, let's hope for the best. This is our chance to show the world what is going on in Iran.

We are officially less than two weeks away from the 2022 FIFA World Cup. I have never seen this sort of divide in Iran concerning this national football team. It must be said, this national football team that used to be our pride has now turned into the Iranian regime's propaganda tool. Today, there has been news that some Iranian football team members have met with Iranian president Ebrahim Raisi.[62] I am particularly disappointed in such actions because it shows that they are not in support of the people. However, we never know the full details. Was this forced? Were they threatened? I believe so. However, it is still disappointing to see that unfold today. The Iranian national football team will now be under fire for many days and weeks to come. They have now lost many supporters for this. Many former Iranian athletes are calling them out.[62] I am conflicted about this situation; this is a team I gave my trust and support for so many years. On one side, these footballers for all we know might be threatened, and do not want further complications. People will be quick to judge, but that should not be a surprise. But on the other side, we are in a situation where we need their voices and support, and they have failed to do so. Of course, this does not apply to the whole team, but rather to those who attended that "meeting".

I will make my decision once we face England, maybe there will be something that they will show to the people of Iran., but now, it is not looking good for this football team.

Iran has lost 6-2 to England. I wish I was kidding. 6-2 is an embarrassing scoreline. I promise you the Iranian national team is not this bad. Regardless of the result, the background behind the game was dark. I woke up at 7 in the morning to watch this game. Players did not sing the national anthem.[63] I was borderline in tears. I am not sure how safe this is for the players, and I can only presume that they will get in trouble leading up to the next game against Wales. I was expecting them to do so. Some people believe that boycotting the national anthem is not enough. This has caused massive traction for the outside world. I have been asked questions by friends about this situation because they were as shocked as I was. At a stage just like the World Cup, not singing a national anthem is a huge issue. Iranian media have censored footage of the team refusing to sing the anthem.[63] Many people in and out of Iran are also celebrating this loss.[63] I must admit, I am still conflicted, I do not know what to make out of this Iran team. We are in a unique situation; I only hope that the whole world got to see a glimpse of what is currently going on in Iran. Usually, I would be annoyed by the score but this time around, I cannot ignore what is going on in my country. It is simply bigger than a game of football.

A part of me is scared for the safety of these players, these actions can lead to worse things. I certainly believe the regime will have a say in this, and it will not be pretty. This World Cup will have to be thrown out of the window; I do not see us doing well anymore.

Despite what went on in that game against England, I believe it is not an entirely bad event. This is a case that will always stay in Iranian history. The fight continues and there is one issue that I want to shed light on. A few days ago, the Iranian regime murdered a 9-year-old by the name of Kian Pirlafak.[64] Kian was a kid that loved engineering. It breaks my heart to know that he will never be able to pursue the dream of becoming an engineer all due to these monsters. However, his name will be remembered and chanted when we will win this battle. I am sure of it. The reason why I want the shed light on this case is to simply show you, dear reader, what this Iranian regime is all about. They are not for the people, and they are willing to kill children to retain power. This is a child-killing regime. Kian is not the only kid to die in these circumstances. On the same night of violence, another 13-year-old child was killed by gunmen.[64] How cruel do you have to be to pull the trigger on innocent children? Unfortunately, it seems that this case will be an ongoing issue and it will not stop until the protests finish. I believe there will be more innocent children dying in the streets of Iran. This is a sentence I never thought I would ever say in my life, but when you come from a place where a murderous regime is out of place, you do not have much of a choice. Many images and videos of people mourning that poor 9-year-old broke my heart, I cannot imagine the pain of the parents, who had a dream for that kid. Imagine how scary it is for the other parents in the country that do not know the future of their children. It is a very scary thought that no one deserves to be in.

Iran has beaten Wales in a World Cup game. I do not think I have been this emotional in a very long time. We beat them in a great way. This game also got political because the Iranian national team chose to sing the national anthem this time.[65] It broke my heart because I was expecting it. Some players looked like they were about to cry singing it and some were barely singing. Whatever it may be, I believe that the Iranian regime had to do with this. I do not know what exactly, but if I had to wonder, I believe that the players' families were most likely threatened. It did look like the players were forced to sing the national anthem. We live in an era where not singing the national anthem is a symbol of resistance and for sure, the Iranian regime did not take that well and had to take the matter into their own hands. The stadium was booing the Iranian national anthem and I was stunned to see that happen, I had never seen that happen on live television. I had one question in my mind, how can these players even perform under such circumstances? The pressure these players must now feel is immense, although they are professional players, there is not much they can now do. In some way, I do feel bad for them, but they had the choice to show their stances long before the World Cup.

I believe that this matter is simply cruel, I believe they should not be in this position. It is a little too much to handle. The repercussions that they would face back home would be tough to swallow, I can imagine.

We just lost against the United States of America in a game of football.[66] I wish I could have worded that sentence differently but unfortunately; it was not meant to be. I do not have the words nor the emotions to explain how frustrated I am with this Iranian football situation. Never have I seen a football team become so divided due to politics. I believe this was meant to be our golden generation and sadly under the Islamic Republic, it has all gone to waste. What I saw on my television after the full-time whistle simply broke my heart. The players gave it all, and they were on the floor crying their eyes out. It was a sad scene to look at. The amount of pressure and abuse that these players have endured makes me feel discouraged. People will not understand, because all they will do is look at the result and not question what is behind it. I hope we can thrive again in football, not only that sport but in all the others. I believe Iranians have so much talent, and it is sad to see that it cannot be displayed properly around the world. However, I must admit, as frustrated as I am for all of this, one part of me is happy that all of this is over. This World Cup was at the wrong time for the country of Iran. We are an unlucky nation; we just must accept it. We seem to never have anything going right for us, it is frustrating. We are at a point in time where we Iranians cannot even enjoy the sport of football. The only positive from this game was how the American players came to comfort the Iranian players at the end of the game, I am sure they must know what is going on in Iran, or at least they should have an idea.

This is what football should be about, peace and unity. Instead in Iran, it is mixed with politics.

A few days have passed since Iran's tragic World Cup elimination in Qatar. It is now time to move on to what is more important in the country. I want to point out an article that came out in the New York Times this week, claiming that the morality police in the country have been "abolished". Of course, this claim is ridiculous and false. My issue with this is how easy it is for Western propaganda to switch up narratives. It now seems that everything is okay in Iran now that the morality police has been "abolished".[67] We all know this is not true, the morality police are one of the millions of problems in Iran. It is not the main one because we have established that the main problem in Iran is the government itself. The morality police are simply a branch of that disgusting regime. Here is what the problem is with this article, for starters, this article is spreading lies and secondly, it is intended to manipulate audiences. Can you see how dangerous that can be?

In other news, TIME magazine has released its heroes of this year, and the mention goes to the women of Iran.[68] I am glad to see some recognition, but I must admit that this achievement does not mean much. This magazine has previously granted Ayatollah Khomeini as the TIME person of the year, which I believe to be ridiculous. Although, they probably did not know any better. Regardless, I hope more media outlets can start picking up the brave work of thousands of Iranian women who are fighting every day for their rights.

Iran's situation is getting worse. There is news of people getting executed due to their protesting of the evil actions of the regime.[69] Here is a friendly reminder that we are in the year 2022. This country is so backward that its judiciary system is not even useful. The Iranian regime executed a 23-year-old named Mohsen Shekari who was linked with attacking a member of the Iranian forces.[69] I believe that execution is not only used as a punishment in Iran. The regime is using this tactic to instill fear in the eyes of the people. Usually, the people that are executed are condemned for "waging war against God".[69] This is simply an excuse for the regime to be able to carry these executions out. This crime of "waging war against God" is simply inhumane in my opinion, I believe that these people are doing no harm. Instead, they are fighting for their rights. I suppose that the Iranian regime is attempting to erase most of its opponents within the country. This is what we call a dictatorship.

These people are as young as me, and it is incredibly worrying to see that nothing is being done by anyone around the world regarding these executions. This is illegal, and there is nothing we can do about it. The international community can sit in their offices and condemn the regime but what good does that do when there is no action? Sanctions do not help the people that are being executed.

It is now New Year's Eve, and I am still quite upset about the executions that are taking place in Iran. I must admit, I have passed the whole day thinking about whether it would be a good idea to have the West involve itself in this revolution. I believe the first step to that would be to dismantle the IRGC. It is no different from the other terrorist organizations that are out there. They are killing hundreds of innocent Iranians and it is also aiding Vladimir Putin in killing innocent civilians in Ukraine. As I have mentioned before, it would be a big policy step-up to class the IRGC as a terrorist group. I am now repeating sentences that I have written a few months ago, and these are thoughts that Iranians all around the world have expressed. There still has been no action taken from any international community. A part of me is slowly starting to lose hope. I do not want to do so, but I do not see any changes coming anymore. What else can the Iranian people do to topple this regime? I will not lose hope, not until the day I die. I will see the Islamic Republic fall. Now that the year is ending, I would like to take the time to give a thought to every Iranian who has passed away this year trying to fight for their rights. I will repeat myself yet again, once this regime falls, the names of the thousands of these angels will be remembered forever.

It may be the start of a new year, but the war against this evil regime is just the beginning. I am expecting Iranians to fight even harder and stronger. We do not have many things in Iran, but the one thing we do have is hope.

We are now in 2023. Hopefully, this is the year when the Islamic Republic finally falls. You may ask yourself if I have any resolutions for the year and to that, I will answer you with one simple phrase: my resolution for the year is for the Islamic Republic of Iran to fall.

Moreover, I also want to try and be a little more politically active, especially on the international stage. I hope this book can help with that. This book is not only for me but also for the thousands of young Iranians that are fighting in the streets of Iran daily just to simply get their voices heard. It is with no doubt that 2022 was a horrible year for Iran. I must admit, it is like any other year. The last 43 years have been abysmal for Iran. Looking back, I suppose it is impressive that my priorities have changed over the course of the year. Fortunately, this publication has captured all of it. It went from speculating how to topple the regime, from the war in Ukraine, to what is going on in Iran nowadays. It will only get worse from here and I am sure that in the next few days, we will hear more horrific news coming out of Iran. I am positive that there will be plenty more executions, murders, and torture and yet again there will be no action from the international community.

Maybe I should not think so negatively, as I mentioned above, maybe this is the year where the IR finally falls. But this is a sentence that I have been telling myself at the start of every single year, and to my surprise, the result at the end of it is always the same.

It is the hope that kills you.

Although the World Cup came to an end a few weeks ago, Iranian football is still targeted by the Iranian regime. An Iranian footballer, Amir Nasr-Azadani has been sentenced to 16 years in prison.[70] His crime? Participating in protests and simply having a different opinion. The regime is telling a different story, these monsters claim that he has been part of the murders of three different security officers.[70] These are all lies because it is a way for the IR to justify their brutal imprisonments which Nasr-Azadani is now another victim of. This is only the beginning; I am sure that the Islamic Republic will try to arrest and imprison not only many other footballers but many talented Iranian athletes. In some way, the IR is killing Iranian sports. My theory on this is very self-explanatory. What athlete can perform when there are hundreds of people dying in the streets of their beloved country? We have all seen what happened at the 2022 FIFA World Cup. A case like this can easily repeat itself in the future, and that is exactly what I fear. Sports is one of many things that the Islamic Republic is stealing from the Iranian people. We cannot even rejoice in the toughest moments with the beauty of sports. The Iranian regime has instated fear in the mind of these athletes, who have all worked hard their whole lives.

What message does this send to the young Iranian athletes, not only in Iran but around the entire world? It is worrying, as we cannot even enjoy something as simple as sports anymore.

Well, this is it. This is the end of this book. I made this book for multiple reasons. As I mentioned at the start, I want to be one of the numerous voices of Iranian youth across the world. This book has covered an experience that a young Iranian has felt abroad. It represents the many feelings, opinions, and viewpoints I have felt and thought about regarding all these matters. My goal is to shed light on the horrors of the Iranian regime all while keeping up to date with world news. Throughout this journey, we have seen some positive light and some terrible news. I must admit, this book would have never been published if it wasn't for the regime. Frankly, I wish I never got to write this. I must also thank my father, who not only inspired me but also pushed me to write this work. I am following in his footsteps, and I hope he, and I will be able to witness the fall of the Iranian regime together. Father, you have worked so hard over the years to get your opinions and frustrations out, and I want to carry that legacy on for the next generation.

You went abroad and escaped the horrors of the IR to give me a better life, and I owe you everything. I have never thought that these events would happen. It goes to show how insane life and politics are. Lastly, I want to finish this work with one last sentence which has been able to reunite Iranians around the globe.

Zan, Zendegi, Azadi.

References

[1] Loveluck, L. (2020, January 3). Iran vows revenge after U.S. Drone Strike Kills Elite Force commander. The Washington Post. Retrieved January 1, 2022, from https://www.washingtonpost.com/world/middle_east/iran-vows-revenge-after-us-drone-strike-kills-elite-force-commander/2020/01/03/345127d6-2df4-11ea-bffe-020c88b3f120_story.html

[2] Thucydides, & Woodruff, P. (1993). On justice, power, and human nature: the essence of Thucydides' history of the Peloponnesian War. Hackett.

[3] Shahrokni, N., & Sofos, S. A. (2022). Mobilizing pity: the dialectics of narrative production and erasure in the case of Iran's #bluegirl. Globalizations, 19(2), 205–219. https://doi.org/10.1080/14747731.2020.1864963

[4] Motamedi, M. (2021). Iran's Supreme leader Khamenei receives local Covid Vaccine. Coronavirus pandemic News | Al Jazeera. Retrieved January 17, 2021, from https://www.aljazeera.com/news/2021/6/25/irans-supreme-leader-receives-local-covid-vaccine

[5] Diba, Farhad. (1986). Mohammad Mossadegh: a political biography. London; Dover, N.H: Croom Helm

[6] Dieterich, H. (1985). Global U.S. State Terrorism: An Interview with Noam Chomsky. *Crime and Social Justice*, *24*, 96–109. http://www.jstor.org/stable/29766271

[7] Almukhtar, S., Peçanha, S., & Wallace, T. (2016, January 5). Behind Stark Political Divisions, a More Complex Map of Sunnis and Shiites. The New York Times. https://www.nytimes.com/interactive/2016/01/04/world/middleeast/sunni-shiite-map-middle-east-iran-saudi-arabia.html

[8] Abrahamian, E. (1989). The Iranian Mojahedin. Yale University Press.

[9] Merat, A. (2018). Terrorists, cultists – or champions of Iranian democracy? The wild wild story of the MEK. The Guardian. Retrieved January 3, 2021, from https://www.theguardian.com/news/2018/nov/09/mek-iran-revolution-regime-trump-rajavi

[10] Tharoor, I. (2021, December 1). Analysis | Is regime change in Iran part of Trump's agenda? The Washington Post. Retrieved January 6, 2021, from https://www.washingtonpost.com/news/worldviews/wp/2018/05/07/is-regime-change-in-iran-part-of-trumps-agenda/

[11] International Institute for Strategic Studies. (2020). Prospects for the Iran nuclear deal. Strategic Comments, 26(8). https://doi.org/10.1080/13567888.2020.1853381

[12] Arafa, M. (2018). A question to the president of the United States, Donald Trump: is it a travel ban, a Muslim ban, or a travel Muslim ban? Revista De Investigações Constitucionais, 5(2), 9–33. https://doi.org/10.5380/rinc.v5i2.58990

[13] Ghazi, M. (2022). Gruesome femicide in Iran. Human Rights Watch. Retrieved February 11, 2022, from https://www.hrw.org/news/2022/02/11/gruesome-femicide-iran

[14] Churchill, R. P. (2018). Women in the crossfire: understanding and ending honor killing. Oxford University Press.

[15] Hakakian, R. (2021). Opinion | A U.N. farce has tragic implications for feminist activists in Iran. The Washington Post. Retrieved February 17, 2022, from https://www.washingtonpost.com/opinions/2021/04/27/un-farce-has-tragic-implications-feminist-activists-iran/

[16] Smith, D. (2008). The state of the Middle East: an atlas of conflict and resolution (Updated 2nd). Earthscan.

[17] Amnesty International. (2021). Iran: Release arbitrarily detained rights activist at imminent risk of flogging. Amnesty International. Retrieved February 20, 2022, from https://www.amnesty.org/en/latest/news/2021/11/iran-release-narges-mohammadi/

[18] Herb, J., Judd, D., Mattingly, P. (2022). Biden condemns 'Russia's unprovoked and unjustified attack on Ukraine' | CNN politics. CNN. Retrieved February 24, 2022, from https://www.cnn.com/2022/02/23/politics/biden-russia-ukraine/index.html

[19] FIFA. (2022). FIFA/UEFA suspends Russian clubs and national teams from all competitions. FIFA. Retrieved March 1, 2022, from https://www.fifa.com/tournaments/mens/worldcup/qatar2022/media-releases/fifa-uefa-suspend-russian-clubs-and-national-teams-from-all-competitions

[20] Evans, S. (2021). Politics and protest in sport: Have FIFA's rules changed? Reuters. Retrieved March 1, 2022, from https://www.reuters.com/article/us-soccer-fifa-protests-idUSKBN2BI2FN

[21] Iskander, N. N. (2021). Does skill make us human? Migrant workers in 21st-century Qatar and beyond. Princeton University Press. https://doi.org/10.2307/j.ctv1nj3437

[22] Adams, C., Essamuah, Z., Walters, S., Abdelkader, R. (2022, March 1). 'Open the door or we die': Africans report racism and hostility trying to flee Ukraine. NBCNews.com. Retrieved March 4, 2022, from https://www.nbcnews.com/news/nbcblk/open-door-die-africans-report-racism-hostility-trying-flee-ukraine-rcna17953

[23] Bella, T. (2022). Putin turns Russia into the world's most-sanctioned country, dwarfing Iran and North Korea. The Washington Post. Retrieved March 8, 2022, from https://www.washingtonpost.com/world/2022/03/08/russia-most-sanctions-putin-ukraine/

[24] Reuters. (2022). Russia says West's sanctions create a 'problem' for Iran Nuclear Deal. Reuters. Retrieved March 8, 2022, from https://www.reuters.com/world/russia-says-wests-sanctions-create-problem-iran-nuclear-deal-2022-03-05

[25] Ismail, A., Davison, J. (2022). Iran attacks Iraq's Erbil with missiles in warning to U.S., allies. Reuters. Retrieved March 13, 2022, from https://www.reuters.com/world/middle-east/multiple-rockets-fall-erbil-northern-iraq-state-media-2022-03-12/

[26] Held to ransom: why has Iran imprisoned Nazanin Zaghari-Ratcliffe? (2017). Economist (United Kingdom), 413 (9064).

[27] Hellyer, H. A. (2022). Opinion | coverage of Ukraine has exposed long-standing racist biases in western media. The Washington Post. Retrieved March 21, 2022, from https://www.washingtonpost.com/opinions/2022/02/28/ukraine-coverage-media-racist-biases/

[28] NATO / Otan. What is NATO? (2022). Retrieved March 23, 2022, from https://www.nato.int/nato-welcome/index.html

[29] Winthour, P. (2022). Russia's belief in NATO 'betrayal' – and why it matters Today. The Guardian. Retrieved March 23, 2022, from https://www.theguardian.com/world/2022/jan/12/russias-belief-in-nato-betrayal-and-why-it-matters-today

[30] WPA Film Library. (1962). Cubans Prepare for War During the Cuban Missile Crisis ca. 1962. [Place of publication not identified]: WPA Film Library.

[31] Iran: Stop covering up sexual assaults in prison. Human Rights Watch. (2009). Retrieved March 27, 2022, from https://www.hrw.org/news/2009/11/06/iran-stop-covering-sexual-assaults-prison

[32] Motamedi, M. (2022). Blame game after Iran women pepper-sprayed at World Cup qualifier. Women's Rights News | Al Jazeera. Retrieved March 30, 2022, from https://www.aljazeera.com/news/2022/3/30/blame-game-after-iran-women-pepper-sprayed-at-world-cup-qualifier

[33] Duerden, J. (2019). Afshin Ghotbi: '1998 had a bigger magnitude for Iranians than Americans'. The Guardian. Retrieved April 1, 2022, from https://www.theguardian.com/football/2019/dec/18/afshin-ghotbi-1998-had-a-bigger-magnitude-for-iranians-than-americans

[34] Breuer, A., Landman, T., & Farquhar, D. (2015). Social media and protest mobilization: evidence from the Tunisian revolution. Democratization, 22(4), 764–792. https://doi.org/10.1080/13510347.2014.885505

[35] Newman, L. H. (2019). How the Iranian government shut off the internet. Wired. Retrieved April 3, 2022, from https://www.wired.com/story/iran-internet-shutoff/

[36] Ensor, J. (2017). Rare public protests spread across Iran amid spiralling inflation. The Telegraph. Retrieved April 3, 2022, from https://www.telegraph.co.uk/news/2017/12/29/rare-public-protests-spread-across-iran-amid-spiraling-inflation/

[37] Erdbrink, T. (2009). Iran election in dispute as 2 candidates claim victory. The Washington Post. Retrieved April 5, 2022, from https://www.washingtonpost.com/wp-dyn/content/article/2009/06/12/AR2009061200916.html?sid=ST2009061104183

[38] BBC. (2009). Iran's presidential candidates. BBC News. Retrieved April 5, 2022, from http://news.bbc.co.uk/2/hi/middle_east/8060304.stm#mousavi

[39] Blair, D. (2015). Hassan Rouhani's glaring failure to curb human rights abuses in Iran. The Telegraph. Retrieved April 5, 2022, from https://www.telegraph.co.uk/news/worldnews/middleeast/iran/11631210/Hassan-Rouhanis-glaring-failure-to-curb-human-rights-abuses-in-Iran.html

40 Al Jazeera. (2021). Iran deporting thousands of Afghan refugees. News | Al Jazeera. Retrieved April 11, 2022, from https://www.aljazeera.com/news/2021/11/11/afghan-refugees-deported-from-iran-as-humanitarian-crisis-deepens

41 France 24. (2022). Iran's Raisi warns Israel against any hostile action. France 24. Retrieved April 18, 2022, from https://www.france24.com/en/live-news/20220418-iran-s-raisi-warns-israel-against-any-hostile-action

42 Al Jazeera. (2022). Israeli forces raid al-Aqsa Mosque, over 150 Palestinians injured. Israel-Palestine conflict News | Al Jazeera. Retrieved April 21, 2022, from https://www.aljazeera.com/news/2022/4/15/israeli-forces-raid-al-aqsa-mosque-over-50-palestinians-injured

43 Charach, K. (2022). Should upcoming soccer friendly between Canada and Iran be cancelled? British Columbia. Retrieved May 17, 2022, from https://bc.ctvnews.ca/should-upcoming-soccer-friendly-between-canada-and-iran-be-cancelled-1.5908102

44 The Canadian Press. (2022). Trudeau says inviting Iran to Vancouver soccer friendly is not 'A very good idea'. CTVNews. Retrieved May 17, 2022, from https://www.ctvnews.ca/politics/trudeau-says-inviting-iran-to-vancouver-soccer-friendly-is-not-a-very-good-idea-1.5906829

45 Burke, A., Tizhoosh, N. (2022). Canada Soccer cancels controversial exhibition game against Iran | CBC News. CBCnews. Retrieved May 26, 2022, from https://www.cbc.ca/news/politics/canada-soccer-cancels-iran-game-1.6466438

46 Gambrell, J., Debre, I. (2022). Crowd confronts Cleric at Iran Tower collapse that killed 33. AP NEWS. Retrieved June 4, 2022, from https://apnews.com/article/iran-middle-east-dubai-united-arab-emirates-building-collapses-56dd92318b631f7ee1d25f1110c9e9a7

47 Caldwell, T., McCreary, K., Sangal, A., Vogt, A., Chowdhury, M., Hammond, E., & Macaya, M. (2022, July 5). July 5, 2022 Highland Park, Illinois, parade shooting news. CNN. Retrieved July 5, 2022, from https://www.cnn.com/us/live-news/illinois-shooting-july-fourth-parade-07-05-22/index.html

48 Tan, Y., Murphy, M. (2022). Shinzo Abe: Japan ex-leader assassinated while giving speech. BBC News. Retrieved July 8, 2022, from https://www.bbc.com/news/world-asia-62089486

49 Gan, N. (2022). Japan's strict gun laws make shootings rare. CNN. Retrieved July 8, 2022, from https://www.cnn.com/2022/07/08/asia/japan-gun-laws-abe-shooting-intl-hnk/index.html

[50] Athas, I., Rizwie, R., John, T., & Ritchie, H. (2022, July 13). Protesters storm Sri Lanka's prime minister's office, as president flees country without resigning. CNN. Retrieved July 15, 2022, from https://www.cnn.com/2022/07/12/asia/sri-lanka-crisis-gotabaya-rajapaksa-airport-intl/index.html

[51] Cowell, A. (2022). Queen Elizabeth II dies at 96; was Britain's longest-reigning monarch. The New York Times. Retrieved September 8, 2022, from https://www.nytimes.com/2022/09/08/world/europe/queen-elizabeth-dead.html

[52] Dahir, A. L., Chutel, L., Peltier, E. (2022). In Africa, the Queen's death renews a debate about the legacy of the British Empire. The New York Times. Retrieved September 9, 2022, from https://www.nytimes.com/2022/09/09/world/africa/queen-africa-british-empire.html

[53] Fassihi, F. (2022). In Iran, woman's death after arrest by the morality police triggers outrage. The New York Times. Retrieved September 17, 2022, from https://www.nytimes.com/2022/09/16/world/middleeast/iran-death-woman-protests.html

[54] Hafezi, P. (2020). Iran's Khamenei says Floyd's killing exposes real nature of U.S. Reuters. Retrieved September 17, 2022, from https://www.reuters.com/article/us-mineapolis-police-iran-khamenei-idUSKBN23A22Z

[55] Yeung, J., Mostaghim, R., Karadsheh, J., Salem, M., Deaton, J. (2022, September 21). Iranian women burn their hijabs as hundreds protest death of Mahsa Amini. CNN. Retrieved September 21, 2022, from https://www.cnn.com/2022/09/21/middleeast/iran-mahsa-amini-death-widespread-protests-intl-hnk/index.html

[56] Fassihi, F. (2022). As Iran cracks down on protests, its president assails 'double standards.'. The New York Times. Retrieved September 21, 2022, from https://www.nytimes.com/2022/09/21/world/iran-ebrahim-raisi-speech.html

[57] Winthour, P. (2022). 'Women, life, liberty': Iranian civil rights protests spread worldwide. The Guardian. Retrieved October 1, 2022, from https://www.theguardian.com/world/2022/oct/01/women-life-liberty-iranian-civil-rights-protests-spread-worldwide

[58] Reuters. (2022). Canada to ban leaders of Iran's Islamic Revolutionary Guards from entry. Reuters. Retrieved October 10, 2022, from https://www.reuters.com/world/canada-ban-irans-irgc-leaders-entry-expand-sanctions-2022-10-07/

[59] Badshah, N. (2022). Blaze at Iran's notorious Evin Prison put out after fight and gunshots reported. The Guardian. Retrieved October 15, 2022, from https://www.theguardian.com/world/2022/oct/15/firefighters-tackling-blaze-at-irans-evin-prison-as-gunshots-reported

[60] Branigan, W. (1978). Terrorists kill 377 by burning theater in Iran. The Washington Post. Retrieved October 15, 2022, from https://www.washingtonpost.com/archive/politics/1978/08/21/terrorists-kill-377-by-burning-theater-in-iran/2eb80ec8-123b-4d73-b351-870bc2a41f3f/

[61] Winehouse, A. (2022). Ukraine FA appeal to FIFA over Iran's inclusion in World Cup. The Athletic. Retrieved October 31, 2022, from https://theathletic.com/3748102/2022/10/31/ukraine-fifa-world-cup-iran/

[62] Motamedi, M. (2022). Iran football legend Daei will not attend World Cup amid protests. Qatar World Cup 2022 News | Al Jazeera. Retrieved November 15, 2022, from https://www.aljazeera.com/news/2022/11/15/iran-football-legend-daei-will-not-attend-world-cup-amid-protests

[63] Whitehead, J. (2022). Iranian state television censors players protesting anthem at World Cup. The Athletic. Retrieved November 21, 2022, from https://theathletic.com/3919310/2022/11/21/iran-world-cup-protest/

[64] Winthour, P. (2022). Iran protests: Family of boy, 9, killed in night of violence blame attack on Security Forces. The Guardian. Retrieved November 22, 2022, from https://www.theguardian.com/world/2022/nov/17/iran-protests-young-boy-among-deaths-night-of-turmoil-mahsa-amini

[65] Whitehead, J. (2022, November 25). Iran sing anthem vs Wales but protests continue. The Athletic. Retrieved November 25, 2022, from https://theathletic.com/3934145/2022/11/25/iran-wales-world-cup-anthem-protests/

[66] Dominski, M. (2022). Follow live reaction after USMNT beat Iran. The Athletic. Retrieved November 29, 2022, from https://theathletic.com/live-blogs/usmnt-vs-iran-world-cup-2022-live-score-updates-result/svs71ZXB8RSo/

[67] Yee, V., Fassihi, F. (2022). Iran has abolished morality police, an official suggests, after months of protests. The New York Times. Retrieved December 5, 2022, from https://www.nytimes.com/2022/12/04/world/middleeast/iran-morality-police.html

[68] Moaveni, A. (2022). Women of Iran: Heroes of the year 2022. Time. Retrieved December 8, 2022, from https://time.com/heroes-of-the-year-2022-women-of-iran/

[69] Motamedi, M. (2022). Iran publicly carries out second protest-related execution. Protests News | Al Jazeera. Retrieved December 17, 2022, from https://www.aljazeera.com/news/2022/12/12/iran-publicly-carries-out-second-protest-related-execution-2

[70] Osborne, S. (2023). Amir Nasr-Azadani: Iranian footballer sentenced to 16 years in prison for taking part in protests. Sky News. Retrieved January 9, 2023, from https://news.sky.com/story/amir-nasr-azadani-iranian-footballer-sentenced-to-16-years-in-prison-for-taking-part-in-protests-12782949

9 798375 385082

www.ingramcontent.com/pod-product-compliance
Lightning Source LLC
Chambersburg PA
CBHW050813250726
48653CB00006B/2206